1897|1997 CNA: A Century of Commitment

CNA and You

CNA celebrated its 100th anniversary in 1997. We could not have reached our centennial milestone without our employees and business partners — you are the backbone of CNA and have been from the beginning. Thanks to you, CNA has become one of the largest, most respected U.S. insurance organizations.

As we take you through CNA's history — our history — we hope to impart the excitement of our dynamic industry and just how vital insurance is to the fabric of society. The passage of time has only strengthened CNA's core values — financial strength, stability and commitment. These values will continue to be the heart and soul of CNA as we meet the challenges of the 21st century.

Employees and business partners together will ensure CNA's continued success as a world-class financial services organization. Thank you for your personal commitment to CNA and all that we stand for.

Dennis Chookaszian
Chairman and Chief Executive Officer
1992 – Present

1897 | 1997   CNA: A Century of Commitment

The year is 1897. Imagine that you work on the railroads, helping to build the networks of steel that are knitting together a dynamic, young nation. You are a skilled and proud worker, an engineer or a conductor. Or, perhaps you earn your salary as a laborer wrestling lengths of rail and wooden ties across the miles. You have a family — a family that depends on your strength.

Now imagine this. One day you are injured on the job or you fall ill with pneumonia. Without warning your world comes crashing down. Who can you turn to? Without insurance coverage, workers have only families or charity to depend upon for their care.

That year an aggressive health and accident insurance company was born — The Continental Assurance Company of North America, now known as CNA.

The new company was incorporated in Hammond, Indiana, with capital stock of $100,000 and a $60,000 surplus to meet claims. Its goals were stated in the original Articles of Association:

The purpose of this Association shall be the making of insurance on the life or health of any person, including the insurance of persons against disability from accidents or sickness.

CNA has come a long way in the 100 years since its inception. Today, CNA is one of the oldest, most respected and most successful insurance companies in America. With more than $60 billion in assets, CNA is one of the nation's largest commercial insurance groups as well as a major property and casualty insurer. CNA broadened its already strong multi-line capabilities through its merger with

Continental Insurance Company in 1995. The company's global capabilities cover risks on land, at sea and in the air, including farmowners' multi-peril, financial risks, inland and ocean marine, personal property and casualty, professional liability for architects, engineers, dentists and nurses, surety bonds, workers' compensation and more.

As CNA embarks on a new century, it is expanding its reach beyond insurance products to insurance-related services that include risk management, information services, health care management and claims administration.

This is the story of CNA…

1897

1920

1897 | 1920 CNA: The Foundation

CNA — The Beginning

Collins Hubbard's kerosene lamp frequently burned into the early morning hours in turn-of-the-century Detroit. The handsome, slightly-built son of one of the city's most prominent families was a dreamer with a businessman's ability to perceive a need in society and the will to fill it.

In 1897, he called together eight of Detroit's leading citizens and presented them with a bold plan to build a powerful and profitable business that would meet one of the city's most pressing needs.

The Detroit Sanitarium was a spacious building complete with elegantly furnished reading rooms, comfortable private rooms, staff nurses who lived on the premises, Turkish and medicinal baths, modern electric appliances, and a kitchen with a full staff. In 1911, after winning a new contract for the Michigan Central Railroad, Continental bought the mortgage on the Sanitarium in order to keep the hospital for the railroad employees.

In Hubbard's day, the insurance business centered on dozens of small regional companies. Most of them offered accident-only coverage. Very few ventured into sickness coverage. Continental was one of the first to accept the challenge.

The plan Hubbard presented to his prospective partners was simple, yet original — to provide America's new working class with a way to survive unexpected disaster. Continental would provide workers with accident and health insurance for a premium of one dollar per month.

To compete successfully, the company offered policyholders a revolutionary option: medical treatment at the Detroit Sanitarium in lieu of a cash settlement. For workers unaccustomed to quality health care, it was an unbeatable offer. Continental purchased the Sanitarium, an outstanding hospital that catered to the city's elite, from the Hubbard family.

Continental's first directors focused on Michigan's railroad workers for their customer base. They also insured vessels, freight, money, goods and other effects — including the insurance of plate glass against loss by breakage — and insurance coverage against fire, lightning, explosion and tornadoes.

After being in business four short weeks, Continental showed assets of $160,718. By the end of that first year of operation, gross premium totaled $156,804, with capital stock of $200,000. Assets increased to $294,527. Two years after its founding, Continental counted 20 railroads among the company's clients, some of them exclusive franchises. By the turn of the century, Continental had become the largest accident insurer in Michigan and had opened additional offices in Indiana, Illinois and Ohio.

Collins Hubbard, the founder of CNA, was born into a prominent Detroit family. Like his father and brother before him, Hubbard seemed destined for a career in law but illness ended his plans to attend Harvard. Hubbard turned instead to the business world.

Industry was booming. Railroads criss-crossed the United States. Factories, particularly in Detroit, turned out cars — the envy of other parts of the world. Hubbard built affordable homes for the workers that were flocking to the Michigan factories. By 1881, at age 31, he was able to purchase property near the center of the city and begin selling apartment buildings. From these activities he accumulated the contacts, capital and business acumen needed to launch the Continental Assurance Company of North America in 1897.

A Company for the New Century

The birth of the new century was a time of invention and explosive growth for the vigorous, young nation. Republican William McKinley won the presidency but fell victim to an assassin's bullet. Vice President Theodore Roosevelt stepped into the Oval Office. Horatio Alger's message — that people can pull themselves up by their bootstraps — infused the national spirit. In 1900, George Eastman introduced the Kodak camera; J. Pierpont Morgan forged U.S. Steel into the world's biggest business; and Samuel Gompers founded the American Federation of Labor to promote the rights of the growing class of industrial workers.

Left
Bright, innovative agents were the cornerstone of Continental's early success.

Below
Eight prominent Detroit businessmen pooled their vision, financial strength, and business savvy, creating the Continental Assurance Company of North America. The company initially occupied a modest two-room office — rooms 409 and 410 — in the Wayne County and Home Savings Bank in Detroit, Michigan.

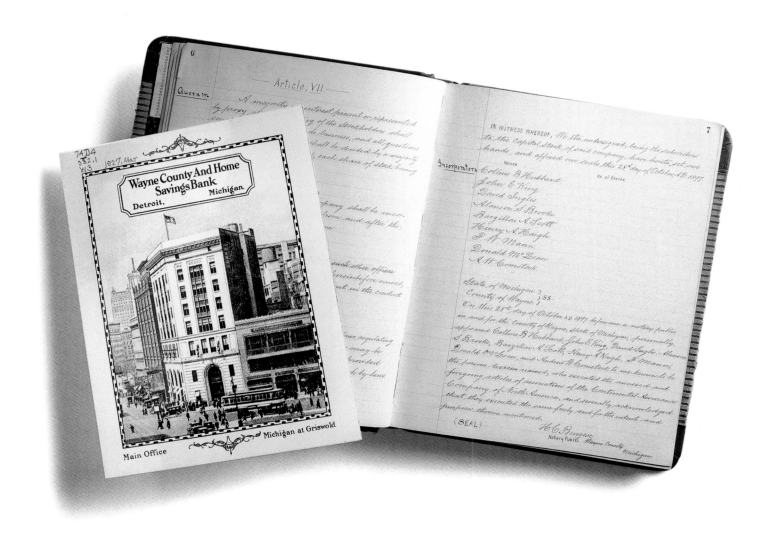

1899

Railroads gained popularity as they afforded a faster and more convenient means of transportation. Unfortunately, the day-to-day operation of locomotives exposed railroad workers to exceptionally dangerous circumstances.

AMONG CASUALTY MEN.

COMBINATION A STRONG ONE.

Continental and Metropolitan Deal Likely to Develop a Strong and Large Western Casualty Company.

The consolidation of the Continental Assurance of Detroit and Metropolitan Accident of Chicago will undoubtedly prove a good move for both companies. It was first broached by General Manager B. A. Scott of the Continental, who did some fine work on the deal. The consolidation retains the name and charter of the Continental, the Continental simply increasing its capital by the $100,000 stock of the Metropolitan and reinsuring the latter.

It occurred to Mr. Scott that both companies could as easily operate under the same plant and largely with the same agency force, and that the business now on the books could be handled better under the consolidation. Before, both companies were comparatively small and young, and not too easy to work with in the field; now an exhibit is made which places the Continental about fifth in the list of accident companies.

In the present case of the Ocean Accident and the Illinois insurance department, in which suit is pending, the Illinois casualty law, providing for the organization of stock companies and under which the Metropolitan was formed, may be declared unconstitutional and there might then have been some complications over the status of the Metropolitan had it continued. By using the Indiana charter of the Continental this possible difficulty is obviated.

It is understood that the company will maintain general offices both at Detroit and Chicago.

The Continental has been a big factor in the railroad accident and health business, but it has never got its hooks in, so to speak, particularly strong in the general accident field.

Continental began its third year in the insurance business with written premium of $200,000. Under the motto, "Protection and Security," the company offered its customers 104 weeks of pay for accidents and 26 weeks for sickness — with coverage of over 200 diseases.

To more accurately reflect the company's mission, the directors of the company voted to change its name from The Continental Assurance Company of North America to the shorter, more forceful Continental Casualty Company (CCC).

A Strong Combination

Despite its rapid growth, Continental was still comparatively small and faced intense competition from other young casualty insurance companies. With an eye toward expansion, the company's first general manager, B.A. Scott, began looking for a partner. He found one in Chicago.

The Metropolitan Accident Company was another small but prosperous insurer. Unlike Continental with its base in the railroad industry, Metropolitan had built its business with manufacturing and industrial workers, offering them a dollar-a-month accident policy similar to Continental's.

In September 1900, the two companies merged retaining the name Continental Casualty. The company then had four departments — railroad, factory, industrial and health. Under the headline, "Combination A Strong One," *The Western Underwriter* reported that the consolidation "will undoubtedly prove a good move for both companies." And it did. Virtually overnight the combined companies vaulted into position as the fifth largest accident insurer in the United States.

The original company logo featured an elegant globe upon which an eagle was perched, holding in its beak a banner bearing the words, "Protection and Security."

1900

CNA's first Chicago office at 134 West Monroe Street was just blocks away from this bustling city scene at the turn of the century.

A Change in Leadership

In 1900, three short years after its incorporation, the original Continental Assurance Company in Detroit merged with two other insurance companies: the Metropolitan Accident Company of Chicago and Railway Officials & Employees Association of Indianapolis.

Leadership of the company was passed from the founder, Collins Hubbard, to Charles H. Bunker, the major stockholder of Metropolitan. It was Bunker who brought in the brilliant H.G.B. Alexander as general manager. H.G.B. Alexander, who had been general superintendent of agencies at Railway Officials & Employees Association, would play a major role in CNA's growth and become its third president in 1906.

Right
Clockwise from top: C.H. Bunker,
Chairman; H.G.B. Alexander, General
Manager; Alan A. Smith, Secretary; and
Franklin H. Head, Treasurer

With the merger, Continental moved to a new home in a new city. Continental's first office in Chicago — at 134 West Monroe Street — consisted of only two rooms. All the details of issuing and servicing policies were handled by three officers and 12 agents. Correspondence was painstakingly handwritten. Policies were entered into a card file. Telephones and electric lights were coming into general use, and most employees commuted to work on horse-drawn street cars.

An Eye Toward Expansion

By 1900 founder Collins Hubbard had turned over the reins of the company to Charles H. Bunker, known to be a man of "rugged integrity," who became the new president as well as majority owner of the company's capital stock. Under Bunker's leadership, Continental launched a strategy of rapid expansion and experienced phenomenal growth. Bunker put agents into 41 states and territories. In order to support his strategy, Bunker poured thousands of dollars of his own money into the company in the form of mortgages and gold bonds, and promised that the company would be "beyond reproach by the insurance commissioners in each state." His efforts paid off. During one month in 1904, nearly 15,000 policies were issued. Bunker stayed at the helm for six years before moving aside for a Continental prodigy — Herbert George Barlow Alexander, fondly referred to as H.G.B.

H.G.B. Alexander is one of the most important figures in the history of CNA. When Alexander joined Continental in 1901 as general manager, the company was writing $225,000 per year in premium. He became president five years later and by the time of his death in 1928, premium income had swelled to more than $13 million per year.

Continental   Casualty

Chicago   Company

Franklin H. Head

OFFICERS OF COMPANY

C. H. Bunker

H. W. Alexander

A. A. Smith

Herbert George Barlow Alexander,
Continental's third president (1906–1928).

H.G.B., an Englishman by birth, decided that greater opportunities lay on the other side of the Atlantic. In the 1880s, he took a job selling accident and health insurance for a small New York City company. It was said that H.G.B. was often up at four o'clock in the morning catching a ride from the neighborhood milkman to the Park Avenue Station of the old New York Central Railroad. He would start the day by selling a policy to a porter or engineer.

Called the "Little Giant" of the casualty world, H.G.B. was a staunch believer in the use of advertising and slogans to keep Continental's name before the public and inspire his work force. He forged a new identity for the company — "Old Reliable Continental" — promising customers, "Our policies are the most fair and liberal." H.G.B. abandoned the original "Globe and Eagle" logo in favor of four interlocking Cs, "The Four Cs" (Continental Casualty Company of Chicago).

One of H.G.B.'s goals was to educate the agents who represented the company. In 1903, he founded a monthly newsletter, the *Continental Agents' Record.* He used the newsletter as a communication tool between the agents and the home office. Alexander believed strongly that an agent could not successfully sell the company's policies unless he could speak intelligently and persuasively about them.

This little pamphlet touted the virtues of CCC, which H.G.B. took great pride in. The brochure appears actual size.

Looking Back with CNA …

After the merger of 1900, the company became the Continental Casualty Company of Chicago and adopted a logo with four interlocking "Cs."

"Success is attainable only

by plain hard work."

— H.G.B. Alexander

The Hustlers

At the turn of the century, Continental had its sales superstars called "The Hustlers." H.G.B. inspired agents by creating a monthly "Hustler's List" of top salespeople and offered prizes and recognition to those who brought in the most new business. Agents who made it to the top of the list had their photos published in the *Continental Agents' Record* and were awarded cash prizes.

One of the first "hustlers" was Theo Schulze, an Illinois native who had worked in the civil service and as a salesman. During his first day on the job, Schulze signed up 19 new customers. He attributed his success to his guiding principle: "Never take 'No' for an answer."

Another Continental All-Star was agent Paul McCaslin. In 1908, McCaslin won entrance to "The Hustler's Club" by becoming Continental's first man to write 100 accident policies. McCaslin was to be awarded a gold watch for his achievement. However, he told the company that he already had a reliable timepiece and did not need further "watching." Instead, he accepted a company check for $100!

Continental — The Trend Spotters

Behind H.G.B. Alexander's gift for advertising and innovation lay a talent for marketing and spotting buying trends. He rapidly moved beyond the company's railroad, manufacturing and industrial base, enabling the organization to grow and profit from new ventures. For example, H.G.B. recognized that women were a vast untapped market for insurance. At his urging, the company was one of the first to underwrite health and accident policies for working women.

The 1904 Hustlers — the upper echelon of the Continental sales force.

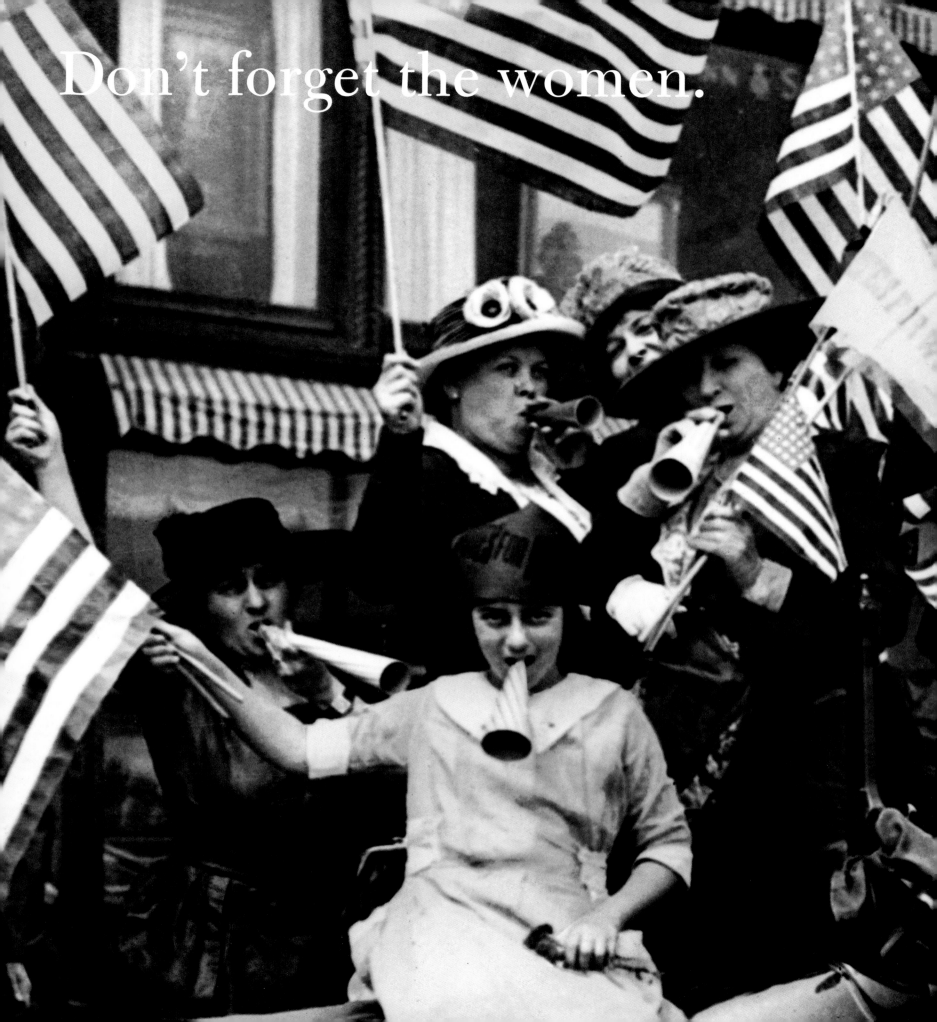

Don't forget the women.

A Continental Casualty Company health and accident policy from 1906 — the premium, $1.10 per month.

"Don't forget," the *Continental Agents' Record* urged, "Continental insures women who have employment from which they derive a regular salary or income." For one dollar per month, female wage earners between the ages of 18 and 45 could sign up for a $25 per month accident indemnity and a $200 accidental death indemnity. Women policyholders were rated "Class W."

Soon after, the company widened its reach to include housewives offering them the same annuity policies available to men — insuring them for loss of life, limb and sight. For five dollars per year, the policy provided up to $6,000 payable over 10 years.

In 1906, Continental became an international insurer by introducing its industrial health and accident policies in London. The British press was skeptical. The *Insurance Index of London* reported that the company was over-reaching itself and predicted that it would have a hard time finding business. Continental fought hard, eliminating the less profitable accidental death line and lowering rates on others.

Continental also launched an innovative new program at home. At that time, lapsed policies were a major problem. Agents at times were too busy to keep track of old business. To combat lapses, the company began sending postcards to policyholders reminding them to renew. The effort was a first for insurance companies and Continental was rewarded with a 50 percent increase in renewed policies.

About this time, Continental was among the first in the industry to notice the birth of a new economic superpower — the middle class. The company stepped in to meet the needs of this emerging class by introducing its first combination policy of both accident and health insurance. The new policy was available to actors, architects, booksellers, shoe sellers, cigar dealers, photographers, schoolmasters and other white collar workers.

Continental paid claimants $1 million in settlements in 1906! The company could proudly claim the title, "The Greatest Health and Accident Insurance Company in the World," promising its customers policies that were "Often copied, never equaled."

At precisely 5:16 a.m. on April 18, 1906, the

ground beneath San Francisco began to shake.

Continental Meets a Challenge

Continental opened a Pacific Coast office in San Francisco in 1905. The office was situated in one of the Bay Area's most modern buildings — 11 stories of fire-proof steel and glass. It was a good location, given what was to come.

At precisely 5:16 a.m. on April 18, 1906, the ground beneath San Francisco began to shake. The shock waves were felt from Los Angeles to Coos Bay, Oregon — a distance of 700 miles. Within a few hours, 50 separate fires broke out and merged into a sprawling mass of flames. Firefighters stood by helplessly — their water mains severed by the quake — as the fire burned for three days and two nights.

The inferno raged through 25,000 buildings and 497 city blocks before it subsided. There were 452 people killed and thousands left homeless. Total damage amounted to $350 million.

The building housing Continental was one of the few in San Francisco's business district that withstood both the earthquake and the fire. The office itself was destroyed but the all-important records were found intact inside the fireproof vaults.

Twenty insurance companies declared bankruptcy as a result of the great quake of 1906. Others sought refuge in loopholes in their policies, which specifically exempted quake damage. However, Continental disdained such practices. It paid every claim on time and in full.

The red area shows the extent of the damage caused by the earthquake.

1906

The San Francisco earthquake and fire
left massive devastation in its wake.

Grand New Offices

Turn-of-the-century Chicago was described by Carl Sandburg as Hog Butcher for the World, Tool Maker, Stacker of Wheat, Player with Railroads and the Nation's Freight Handler, Stormy, Husky, Brawling, City of the Big Shoulders.

Educator John Dewey; retail magnate Marshall Field; crusading journalist Upton Sinclair; humorist Finley Peter Dunne; and civil rights pioneer Ida B. Wells were among the men and women walking the streets of Chicago in those days. Sears, Roebuck and Company was emerging as the nation's leading retailer. Frank Lloyd Wright's Prairie School architecture was attracting world-wide attention. Civil engineers had recently completed a massive project to reverse the flow of the Chicago River to save both Lake Michigan's purity and Chicago's water supply.

American author Theodore Dreiser wrote: "Chicago's many and growing commercial opportunities gave it widespread fame … The sound of the hammer engaged upon the erection of new structures was everywhere heard. Great industries were moving in."

Continental grew along with Chicago — so rapidly, in fact, that by 1905 it had outgrown its headquarters. Construction began on a new four-story building at 1208 South Michigan Avenue. It boasted "Chicago Windows" that dominated the entire facade of the building and let in the maximum amount of light through their large, rectangular planes.

The new headquarters stood as a powerful and tangible symbol of Continental's success. Its modern, open plan with one large room in the center of the building and galleries along each side provided private offices for each manager, as well as an in-house bank, post office and telephone exchange. Said one critic, "The Continental Casualty Company surely has grand, new offices."

Above
A postcard heralding Chicago as a city for the new century.

Right
Continental moved into its prestigious new headquarters, signaling its rapid growth, burgeoning financial strength and reputation.

Continental Agents' Record

Seventh Year   CHICAGO, ILLINOIS, SEPTEMBER, 1910   No. 74

ENLARGED HOME OF THE LARGEST HEALTH AND ACCIDENT INSURANCE COMPANY IN THE WORLD

(From a photograph taken August 16, 1910.)

"The Best Equipped Casualty Company Building in the World"

Harvey H. Shomo, Secretary of the American Casualty of Reading, interviewed many Detroit Conference members on the arrangement and equipment of their offices. Mr. Shomo will visit the plant of the Continental Casualty in Chicago and other company home offices this fall.

The Continental has probably the best equipped casualty company building in the world.—*The Insurance World*, Pittsburg, August 2, 1910.

Hog Butcher for the World, Tool Maker, Stacker of Wheat, Player with Railroads

the Nation's Freight Handler, Stormy, Husky, Brawling, City of the Big Shoulders.

— Carl Sandburg

Expanding Into Multiple Lines

By 1910 one million people had been helped by Continental. George Schwartzbower, a locomotive fireman from Melrose, South Dakota, received $780 for a back injury. Chicago cashier Otto Krause was given $125 after coming down with a bad case of "la grippe" — now commonly known as the flu. Sarah Cain, a seamstress from Port Jervis, New York, was paid $95.80 after suffering a spinal injury.

The time had come for Continental to move beyond its core businesses of health and casualty insurance and become more customer focused and responsive to market demands. In 1910, the directors voted to assume more risk by greatly expanding the company's product lines. Continental added hospitalization, fidelity, surety, inland marine, burglary and auto insurance. The new initiatives succeeded. Not long after, agents presented $80,000 in new business to H.G.B.

With net premium income topping $3 million a year, the company was strong enough to take another big step — into the life insurance business. Continental Assurance Company (CAC) was created and on August 15, 1911, issued its first policy. Continental Assurance operated independently of the casualty company, though it was managed by the same board of directors and had the same president, H.G.B. Alexander. It was licensed in 11 states and the District of Columbia.

An early customer was William F. Bagnell of Colorado. Bagnell was killed in an automobile accident on August 28, 1912. His beneficiary received $12,000 on his three-year-old CAC policy.

Continental Casualty Company was not allowed to sell life insurance under the terms of its original charter and the laws of various states. In order to sell life insurance, a new company had to be created. Five of the CCC directors founded a separate company in April 1911, naming it Continental Assurance Company, a title taken from the original founding company. The directors who put up the $150,000 for the new company were H.G.B. Alexander, W.H. Roberts, Landon C. Rose, R.I. Stearns and Arthur W. Underwood. H.G.B. Alexander served as president of both companies.

By 1913, when the life insurance company was solidly on its way, the original stockholders were able to transfer ownership to CCC, realizing from the transaction exactly the amount they collectively advanced to get the Continental Assurance Company started.

H.G.B. Alexander's "Welcome Back Day."

Agents welcomed back Continental's vacationing president with applications worth $80,000 in premiums.

One of the fledgling life insurance company's first sales stars was a woman of "remarkable energy … and quiet dignity," Miss Helen V. Barnhart. Miss Barnhart was among the first women to move from behind the typewriter into the sales force. She became very successful and wrote more than $100,000 in life insurance policies in one year. Her success qualified her for membership in the Assurance's prestigious 1–2–0 Club of top sellers — the first woman ever accepted into the club.

Left
As the number of automobiles on the roads increased, so did the number of driving accidents. Continental again responded to the insurance needs of the public, moving into automobile liability insurance.

Right
Miss Helen Barnhart attended a convention in Indiana with other members of the 1–2–0 Club.

Advertising Pays Off

H.G.B. Alexander wanted to make the Continental "brand" familiar in every household and he knew just how to do it — with advertising.

H.G.B. launched two major advertising campaigns in the years prior to World War I. The most famous of them, the Continental clock, appeared regularly in newspapers and magazines across the nation. The company proudly boasted

Rain or shine, every time the clock ticks, every working hour, the Continental Casualty Company, Chicago, pays a dime to somebody, somewhere, who is sick or hurt.

Agents were urged to make the Continental clock "as familiar and as welcome as the sunshine or a mother's kiss."

Continental's advertising department also created "The Red Book," a booklet for agents' use that explained the full line of Continental products in laymen's terms. This exceptional marketing tool carried the slogan, "Better Have Something for a Rainy Day." The trade journal, *Insurance Press of New York,* called the pamphlet a "must read" … filled with sensible light reading and prepared in an attractive style.

By 1912, the Continental was paying more than 50,000 claims per year. When selling to tough customers, the company advised its agents

When a prospect says to you, "Oh, I don't expect to get hurt; my work isn't dangerous," the very best answer you can give him is to show him how many claims your company has recently paid to men doing exactly the same sort of "safe" work.

BETTER HAVE SOMETHING FOR A RAINY DAY

By 1911, the company boasted that, "every 2 minutes, 26 seconds, Continental Casualty Company breaks somebody's fall from safety and good health with a soft layer of cash indemnity."

RAILROAD DEPART[MENT]

STOP-LOOK-LISTE[N]

FULL SPEED AHEAD.

Biggest, Best and Easiest Prize Competition Yet.

By the time this issue of the Record reaches the Railroad Installment Department representatives they will have received the announcement of the Fall Contest for which they have been waiting for some time.

The Contest this year will be along practically the same lines as previous ones, but in order to avoid any possibility of the interest lagging because of its length, the management decided to shorten the Contest period one month, thereby concentrating the work incident to such competitions to the last quarter of 1911.

The prizes will be awarded on a basis of comparison with results of the third quarter (July-August-September) of 1911. There will be five "Divisions," where there were three before, and **fifteen** "Division Prizes" (three in each Division), where there were but twelve similar prizes before.

In addition to the fifteen "Division Prizes," there will be offered:

Three Prizes of One Hundred Dollars Each:

One Hundred Dollars to the representative who [during the Contest pe-]

SPIKES AND TIES

9

NT

ER

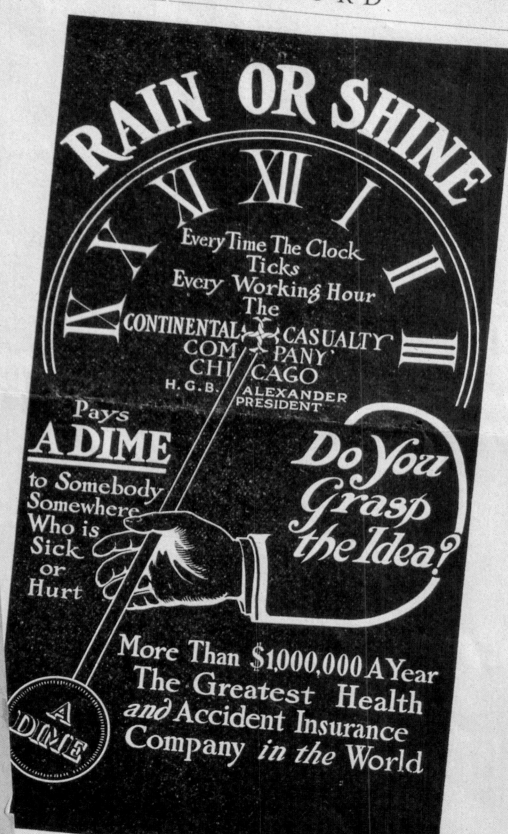

Continental's new offices at 910 South Michigan Ave. were equipped with the latest technological advances. Shown here are an addressograph (left) and addressograph graphotype, which employees used to address policyholder mailings.

The company manual listed 5,000 occupations with the reminder that, "no man is safe; none is immune from accidents and illness, no matter what his occupation is, and we have the proof in our Claim Department records." Records show that in 1912, Continental paid claims of $2,458 to 124 ice wagon drivers, $105,828 to 1,238 railroad engineers, $973 to 77 laundresses, and $2,795 to 131 police patrolmen.

On Top as Always

In 1915, the *Continental Agents' Record* announced the big news — that expansion had once again forced the company to seek new offices. Continental, in its new headquarters at 910 South Michigan Avenue, occupied the top floor of a 12-story building. As the *Continental Agents' Record* put it, Continental's new headquarters were "on top as always, and right in the middle of things."

The new headquarters boasted the latest in office technology to efficiently serve the company's 200,000 policyholders and 5,000 agents. Telephones connected the desks of all department heads. Gone were the roll-top desks of old. The new desks were all of the flat-top variety which, according to the *Continental Agents' Record,* "reveal so plainly at the end of each day's work whether everything is cleaned up or not!" Within a few years, the company added electric postage machines, capable of handling 250 letters a minute. Stamps at that time cost two cents and four cents.

Taking the Lead in Service

Continental saw another opportunity to expand beyond its "bread and butter" lines of health and accident insurance by moving into the emerging field of workers' compensation. It joined two other companies in an experiment. Each company agreed to reinsure workers' compensation policies written by the others, with Continental taking 50 percent of the business and accepting a maximum liability of $2,500 for injury to an individual.

The move put Continental into direct competition with various state insurance funds. But the company's firm belief that private insurance could compete effectively with government funds was borne out — so much so that by 1915 the Continental formed a separate workers' compensation department. The company also announced that it was dropping all restrictive clauses in the policies as old-fashioned and out of touch with customers' needs.

Continental's famous Golden Rule policy provided "complete protection without question or quibble backed by years of company reputation." Under the Golden Rule, the company promised to bear the full financial burden for any loss from sickness or accident. This policy was a bit more expensive, but the increasingly affluent middle class proved willing to pay a premium price for a premium policy.

A Token Payment

The "biggest insurance deal of the century" was sealed with a penny on December 31, 1916. For years, Continental had a franchise with the Union Pacific Railroad under which it had exclusive rights to provide employees with health and accident insurance. However, in 1916, Continental, in alliance with The Equitable Life Assurance Society, dropped the franchise in favor of a group policy.

The negotiations behind the biggest insurance deal of the era were revealed in the memoirs of William J. Graham, a director of Equitable. For months, representatives of the two insurance companies had been working to close the deal. Finally, on New Year's Eve, they signed an agreement with Charles B. Seger, the Union Pacific's CEO. Only one detail remained — a token payment. Graham recounted

He asked me what I had in mind. I suggested that a payment of $1,000 might be sufficient. He reached into his pocket and said, "Well, now, I realize that insurance is commonly paid in advance of the time when it becomes effective. But I haven't $1,000 — we are closed down for the year. However, I want to make a payment." And he took a penny from his pocket and handed it to me, saying, "Here is a token payment."

For that penny payment, the Union Pacific's 41,000 employees were automatically insured — at no cost to themselves — against sickness and accident, and given life insurance regardless of age, occupation or physical condition. The total amount of insurance was $30 million at a cost to the railroad of about $800,000 a year.

Continental's first successful group insurance deal dramatically changed the way the company did business. No longer did agents have to solicit individual employees. From this time forward, business was increasingly conducted with the employer.

When the United States entered World War I, the Union Pacific deal made headlines again. President Woodrow Wilson took possession of the nation's railways to ensure the swift and efficient delivery of war supplies to the Eastern seaboard for shipment to Europe.

In effect, all railway workers became government employees at the stroke of a pen. There was one problem: none of the other railroad companies offered their employees the kind of generous insurance plan available at the Union Pacific. Therefore, the government decided to cancel the Union Pacific's group plan.

Executives of the two insurance companies rushed to Washington to plead their case, pointing out that canceling the popular plan could spark labor unrest. The federal government eventually agreed and reentered the agreement. This was the first time that Washington became involved in the group insurance field.

In April 1917, one month after his inauguration, President Wilson asked Congress to declare war on Germany, proclaiming, "The world must be made safe for democracy."

Over There

On June 28, 1914, an assassin's shots rang out in the streets of Sarajevo, ending the life of Archduke Francis Ferdinand, Crown Prince of Austria. Within months, all of Europe was at war.

At first, the war overseas had little impact on the United States. In 1914, the nation was in the grip of an economic recession. Factories were shutting down and laying off their workers. The economic downturn hit Continental Casualty Company hard. But, it hit back, announcing a new "Popular Policy" with a dollar-a-month premium. To win customers, the Popular waived chronic disease clauses and probationary illness periods.

Archduke Francis Ferdinand in Sarajevo.

1917

During World War I, women replaced men in most industries, including automobile building and repair.

To help the company weather the hard times, officers agreed to a voluntary reduction in salary. Continental also stepped in to help its employees. That year, the company gave Christmas bonuses — 10 percent of one month's salary — to everyone who earned less than $100 per month. H.G.B. Alexander also offered cash prizes to top sellers. First prize was $50.

With America's entry into World War I in 1917, factory production boomed once again. The entire nation mobilized. Sixty-one men from Continental's home office rushed to enlist. On the home front, employees plunged into the war effort, purchasing Liberty Loan Bonds and collecting thousands of dollars for organizations like the YMCA and the Red Cross.

As men left for the front, women took their places in the work force. In recognition of their new role, Continental announced that all women who took over traditional male jobs would be insured in the same way as men. "The patriotic response of the women of this country should be encouraged," the company announced, stating further that women "should, in so far as possible, receive the same kind of income protection as male risks."

And what of the soldiers? Continental announced that it would pay all death claims arising from military or naval service regardless of policy provisions exempting such deaths.

The company also refunded all war service premiums — those extra payments made by service men who wanted to maintain their life insurance policies despite joining up.

The Honor Roll paid tribute to Continental men fighting during World War I.

ROLL of HONOR

Ashmore, J. C.
Asperger, O.
Bain, E. H.
Baumann, C. J.
Burnelle, H. E.
Byrne, H. R.
Carlson, H. W.
Clark, E. A.
Clark, H. A.
Cords, E. H.
Dabney, W. B.
Deweese, B. M.
Dorn, R. W.
Duck, B. C.
Evans, D. W.
Farris, J. M.
Hamilton, R. R.
Harder, P. E.
Hayslett, W. G.
Higgins, T.
Hug, E. J.
Hynds, H. D.
Jackson, L. H.
Jennett, R.
Johns, S.
Jones, H. W.
Kersting, A. A.
Kersting, A. V.
King, E. S.
Kraft, H.

Lambert, E. E.
Lodge, W. M.
Lough, C. M.
McGehee, S.
McEvoy, J. S.
Mader, W. A.
Maris, H. R.
Masich, R.
Mason, W. J.
Miller, H. T.
Morrissey, N. E.
Nassau, J.
Pearman, R.
Polanek, F.
Ringwalt, L. B.
Roberts, F. M.
Roe, M.
Schramek, W. J.
Schwartz, J.
Smiley, M.
Talley, F. H.
Tinsley, J. W.
Tuchbreiter, R.
Ulmar, S.
Underwood, P.
Watkins, W. W.
Webb, P. G.
Welter, R. C.
Whitchurch, C. A.
Williams, A. H.
Wilson, H. J.

1920

1950

Continental Casualty's Roaring '20s

America emerged from World War I with a roar! It was the jazz age — a time of frenzied action fueled by bootleg whiskey and an unquenchable zest for living, a time of hedonism and rampant materialism.

The decision that defined the age came in the first month of the decade. With the Volstead Act, America officially became "dry." In Chicago, Prohibition ushered in an era of flappers and speakeasies, gangsters and tommy guns. Al Capone became the city's most prominent and powerful citizen, overshadowing others like Clarence Darrow, Louis Armstrong and writers Ben Hecht and Charles MacArthur.

In 1920, 2.7 million people called Chicago their home. Across America cities were achieving dominance over rural areas, and the Model T was speeding across the cities and countryside. Radio took to the air. KYW became Chicago's first station in November of 1921. Over the course of the decade, Soldier Field officially opened, construction work began on the Merchandise Mart, and the Bears moved to Wrigley Field. By 1924, 30,000 factories were turning out $7 billion worth of goods. The average wage — about $15 a week.

America's can-do spirit of innovation and excitement was felt throughout Continental. By 1923, Continental had become a major casualty company, with operations extending into every state in the United States and every province in Canada.

A New Generation of Leadership

By the 1920s, H.G.B.'s decision to expand beyond health and accident into multiple lines was beginning to pay off. The intensity of the decade sparked a flurry of ideas for products targeted to the needs of America's increasingly powerful and affluent middle class and the businesses it supported. To develop the new lines and expand operations, H.G.B. made Herman A. Behrens general manager of the two companies in 1923.

Behrens, a seminal figure in CNA history, was a lifelong insurance man. His father was an actuary and he became one, too. Behrens was a phenomenon. He arrived in Chicago at the age of 24 to set up an office for a small California-based insurance company and by the age of 29 was offered a vice presidency at Continental Casualty.

In 1924, the allegorical representation of justice was adopted by the company as the new trademark.

HERMAN A. BEHRENS
1883 • 1945

H.A. Behrens was president of both CCC and CAC after H.G.B. Alexander's death in 1928. From 1935 to 1945, he was also chairman. He served his country during World War I as deputy commissioner at the Bureau of War Risk Insurance. In his private life, he loved photography and yachting.

"... a relationship doesn't just happen. It results

from right thoughts and hard work by all of us."

— Herman A. Behrens

APRIL IS "AUTOMOBILE INSURANCE" MONTH

SELL MORE
AUTOMOBILE INSURANCE

HOW?   WHERE?   WHY?

SEE INSIDE PAGES

The *National Underwriter* described Behrens as a man of "utmost resourcefulness … genial and an attractive comrade … possessed of enormous energy … yet never strident or obviously aggressive." His genius lay in his organizational abilities and his willingness to allow agents a high degree of independence.

In fact, Behrens, with H.G.B.'s support, was instrumental in turning Continental into the "agent's company." He would sometimes leave the office for weeks at a time, allowing his people the opportunity to grow by carrying on without him. He also provided business tips and guidance, developing a synergy between the home office and the field, ensuring that there was no mysterious barrier between agents and the folks at headquarters. The following is typical of his managerial style. In 1922, then-Vice President Behrens circulated a letter giving agents 60 days advance notice of a rate increase. Such notice had never been given before. It allowed field representatives — before the rate hike — to mount a whirlwind campaign, which resulted in record-breaking sales.

GAMA

In September 1924, managers of the Continental Assurance Company sat down with 22 independent agents to trade advice, opinions and bad jokes. It was the founding meeting of GAMA, the General Agents and Managers Association.

GAMA was the company's first attempt to set up a formalized dialogue with executives and the people who sold the policies. It served as an advisory body to the life company and provided a forum in which company managers and agents could openly discuss and resolve problems concerning policies, services and distribution. GAMA also educated and trained agents, helping turn jobs into professions.

The sharing of information through GAMA helped both the company and the sales force. Better-informed agents were able to better serve customers which, in turn, increased both CNA's sales and its prestige in the industry.

GAMA became the model for future agent advisory councils like PACER, which was formed in 1967 for property and casualty agents.

Left
By the middle of the decade, auto insurance was CCC's biggest line of business.

Right
GAMA's logo by 1997.

Bolts and Bars cannot a...
Sell your clien...

THIS IS A REPRINT OF ADVERTISEMENT WHICH APPEARED IN THE INS

EARED IN THE INSURAN

protection fro
urglary insur

Engagement rings
insured under a S
America Fore po
Rate: 2½ %
Minimum Premium $

75

Smiling Bill

On November 22, 1927, the unfortunate Charles A. Thistlethwaite of Ilion, New York, was hit by a car and died. At the time of his death, he was carrying Continental's Special Automobile Double Indemnity policy, Form 237A. Mr. Thistlethwaite had paid a total of $123 dollars in premium over three years. Thanks to his foresight — and Continental's new policy — his widow was awarded a payout of $24,000 — a return of some 2,000 percent!

By the late 1920s, auto accidents and pedestrian injuries had emerged as the two greatest exposures in the accident field. To decrease the number of auto and pedestrian claims, Continental agents turned to Smiling Bill.

Smiling Bill was a big, hearty policeman who specialized in teaching children traffic safety — this at a time when thousands of schoolchildren were killed by cars every year. Smiling Bill lived, by the way, within the pages of a comic book!

The Smiling Bill Safety Campaign was launched in 1928 and it worked like a charm. Continental agents distributed booklets containing colorful safety tips to kids in the community. After reading the comic book, a child was recognized as a Smiling Bill Safety Helper and was awarded a nickel-plated star to wear. The catch was those stars were delivered by hand to each child's home by a Continental agent!

Multiple Lines Pay Off

Behrens knew that the accident and health (A&H) department was the backbone of the company. But he also knew the importance of being a multiple line insurer, and his primary goal was to inspire agents to diversify by selling Continental's many new policies. Among the most important of these was liability insurance.

Continental's new offerings included

Auto liability policies. By 1921, more than nine million automobiles were on America's roads. In Chicago alone, police records logged 126 motor vehicle fatalities in one three-month period. For every person killed, another 20 were injured. Continental was the only company to issue a personal accident policy in conjunction with auto liability coverage. By mid-decade, auto insurance had emerged as Continental's biggest line.

General and homeowners liability lines. "Slip and fall" policies were designed to protect against third-party injury. Homeowners liability policies included coverage for theft and larceny. The company also created its first policy covering valuables — such as gold, precious stones, silver, jewelry and furs — which offered a coinsurance clause that split liability with the customer.

Bank, burglary and embezzlement policies. Continental Casualty was one of the first companies to underwrite bank robbery risks, including coverage for the contents of safe deposit boxes. The company also offered surety and fidelity policies to protect against embezzlement by employees. Its lines were extensive and included coverage against safe burglary, interior and exterior holdup, residence burglary, safe deposit box theft, and paymaster holdup.

Liability insurance was not the only innovation that fueled Continental's growth during the Roaring '20s. In 1921, CAC introduced the Bank Plan which, in cooperation with local banks, allowed policyholders to obtain a mix of savings and life insurance and encouraged bank savings. Within 10 years, the Bank Plan put $35 million in life insurance on the books. Continental Assurance also introduced the revolutionary Salary Investment Plan, one of the nation's first payroll deduction programs. By 1923, thanks to its group insurance contract with the Cleveland Teachers Association, Continental could claim the first association group policy ever written by an insurer.

1927

In May 1927, Charles A. Lindbergh completed a solo flight across the Atlantic and became a hero to millions. CCC quickly recognized a new niche and began to offer accident coverage for pilots and planes.

Continental Takes to the Skies

In the late 1920s, Americans were taking to the highways by the millions but they also were taking to the skies. And, Continental took wing with them.

It was the age of Lucky Lindy and the first transatlantic flight. Amelia Earhart was in the air. Daring pilots were setting records: New York to Germany in 43 hours; the first flight between San Francisco and Honolulu; the first flight over the South Pole.

The Continental companies were quick to recognize that a new industry was being born, and equally quick to design new policies to capture that industry. Operating under the principle of what comes up must come down, agents were urged to sign up policyholders both in the air and on the ground through a newly acquired subsidiary, The National Casualty Company, in collaboration with another company, National Fire of Hartford.

In the air, The National Continental Aviation Insurance Association offered accident and fire coverage for planes and pilots. On the ground, customers could purchase general liability and property damage coverage.

An Educated Work Force

With the variety of new policies being issued by both Continental Casualty and Continental Assurance, the companies faced a problem. The agents were having difficulty keeping up with the number and diversity of new products: general and homeowners liability, aviation, surety and fidelity, and salary investment plans, just to name a few. It was time to return to school.

In September of 1925, Continental announced that it was founding a training program for underwriters. The first training director, Roy LeFevre Davis, was described as "a lifelong proponent of the theory of learning while selling."

According to the *Continental Agents' Record,* the school had two purposes: to give Continental agents a thorough education in the theory and practice of salesmanship; and to ground them in the fundamentals of insurance in all of its branches.

The agents' training course lasted three weeks and mixed class-room instruction with field work. Topics included functions of life insurance, principles of policy contracts, and methods of selling. The agents' school even provided scripts to play-act. One early scenario allowed agents to take on the roles of Mr. Salesman and his customer, Mr. Harold Carlson, a family man about 32 years old.

Reprinted from "Printers' Ink"

Salesman: *Hello, Mr. Carlson, how are you today? (They shake hands.)*

Carlson: *Never felt better in my life. If you think you are going to sell me more life insurance, you will have to come back some other time since I am flat broke.*

Salesman: *Don't get scared, Mr. Carlson (smiling), I came to make you a present of something that will mean dollars and cents to you and your family someday.*

Carlson: *That sounds good. What's the joke?*

Needless to say, by the time Mr. Salesman had finished, he had won over Mr. Carlson. But not only the agents gained from going back to school. Customers benefited as well by being able to rely on trained advisers versed in the latest offerings.

Continental produced manuals such as these to keep agents informed about new lines of business.

Putting Employees First

During the 1920s, Continental proved that it was also concerned about the well-being of its employees.

In 1921, H.G.B. Alexander devised a bold plan to tie the success of the company to the individual successes of its people. He announced a plan to issue $200,000 in new common stock to be sold exclusively to agents and employees.

"The only way I could expect to succeed in a large way would be by helping others," H.G.B. said. "My theory was that it is more blessed to give than to receive and as a result of a great deal of thought along that line, I figured that I could arrange to release some stock so that associates who worked so diligently and ably for the company, and had contributed to its success, would have the opportunity of becoming part owners."

About the same time, the Continental companies created The Continental Welfare Association, which offered workers free disability pensions, life insurance, retirement pensions — and for women, a wedding allowance of $20 for each year of service! But Continental was interested in more than just the financial well-being of employees. It launched a series of family-oriented social programs as well — annual picnics, weekend retreats, dances, and outdoor activities for employees and their families.

As the *Continental Agents' Record* put it

A wedding allowance for her, if she marries.
Tea, dances and a pension if she stays single.
What can a poor girl do?

In a time of labor turnover and half-hearted service, the *Insurance Press of New York* reported that Continental's welfare plan helped it "steadily outgrow cobwebbed contemporaries."

Opposite page, bottom
Continental began competing with other company baseball teams in 1908. By the 1930s, they were playing in city-wide leagues composed of more than 300 teams.

Other photographs
The Continental Welfare Association sponsored picnics, weekend retreats, dances and outdoor activities for employees and their families.

The Peaches

From its earliest days, CNA has made a commitment to women in the workplace. The first female employees served mainly as clerks and typists. But in the years following World War I — when women began taking new jobs in large numbers — female agents were among the company's top sellers. In fact, as early as the 1920s, Continental was actively recruiting women with the promise, "there is no field in the business world that affords greater opportunities to women than the solicitation of insurance."

In the 1920s, CNA's high-achiever female agents were nick-named "Peaches" and spotlighted in the monthly *Continental Agents' Record.*

One such Peach was Helen Doyle of Continental Casualty. In 1927, the *Record* praised her "bulldog tenacity." "Doyle," it reported, "will keep after a risk in a pleasant and most polite way and never gives up. She proves that a woman has a place in business."

Peach Ida Handel, was another sales leader. In 1928, Handel sold more than $100,000 in life insurance in her first six months on the job. In the month of April alone, she closed 36 policies for a total of $45,000 in insurance. The *Record* reported: "Ida was shy at first, but through her work, she has acquired new poise, confidence and self-assurance."

Peach Helen Barnhart, disclosed her secret of success as one of CNA's early female agents: "Making other women feel and know that I, as a woman, have their insurance problems seriously at heart, and can intelligently and sympathetically advise them."

Business blooms all year 'round for them in Life, Accident and Health, Special and General Lines. Who said Beauty and Brains didn't go together?

The Baton Is Passed

For nearly three decades, one visionary had guided Continental, taking the company from a small accident and health insurer to a large, multi-line insurance business. In recognition of his many contributions, H.G.B. Alexander was named Continental Casualty's first chairman of the board in early 1928. It was to be his final honor. In October of that year, the news flashed from Paris — the Little Giant of the casualty world had died while touring Europe with his wife and daughter. As the sad news spread throughout the company, H.G.B. Alexander was praised as "a man of penetrating vision, splendid judgment and [possessing] a most happy gift of being able to measure a man's ability."

With H.G.B.'s death, the baton of leadership passed to Herman A. Behrens, whose 17-year stewardship would steer the company through the Great Depression and another world war. Behrens was named president and later became chairman of the board in 1935.

In 1929, GAMA presented an elegant clock, made of carved walnut, as a memorial to H.G.B. Alexander. "It was to be a tribute of love, high esteem and friendship to the man who so successfully guided the Continental companies for a number of years," pronounced Ten Broek, GAMA's president. The clock, which stands a little more than 7.25' tall, has a 13" base and is 18 inches at its widest point, now stands in the office of Dennis Chookaszian, chairman and chief executive officer of CNA.

Upon H.G.B. Alexander's death in 1928, Vice President and General Counsel Manton Maverick wrote this tribute on behalf of officers, agents and employees.

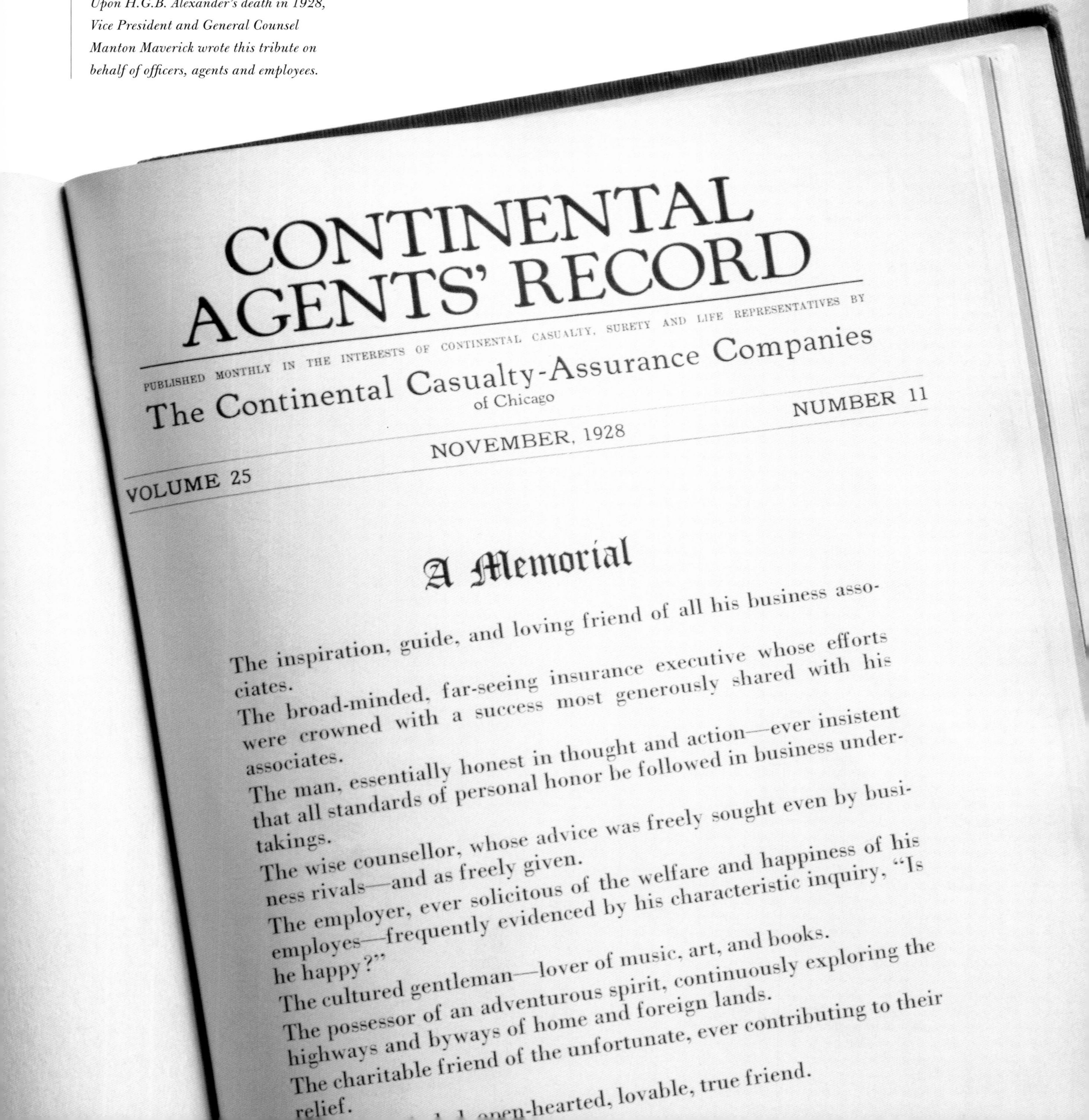

CONTINENTAL AGENTS' RECORD

PUBLISHED MONTHLY IN THE INTERESTS OF CONTINENTAL CASUALTY, SURETY AND LIFE REPRESENTATIVES BY

The Continental Casualty-Assurance Companies
of Chicago

VOLUME 25 NOVEMBER, 1928 NUMBER 11

A Memorial

The inspiration, guide, and loving friend of all his business associates.

The broad-minded, far-seeing insurance executive whose efforts were crowned with a success most generously shared with his associates.

The man, essentially honest in thought and action—ever insistent that all standards of personal honor be followed in business undertakings.

The wise counsellor, whose advice was freely sought even by business rivals—and as freely given.

The employer, ever solicitous of the welfare and happiness of his employes—frequently evidenced by his characteristic inquiry, "Is he happy?"

The cultured gentleman—lover of music, art, and books.

The possessor of an adventurous spirit, continuously exploring the highways and byways of home and foreign lands.

The charitable friend of the unfortunate, ever contributing to their relief.

open-hearted, lovable, true friend.

This memorial plaque paid tribute to H.G.B. Alexander.

Then, on October 29, 1929 — a day forever known as Black Tuesday — investors

dumped 16 million shares onto the New York Stock Exchange at declining prices.

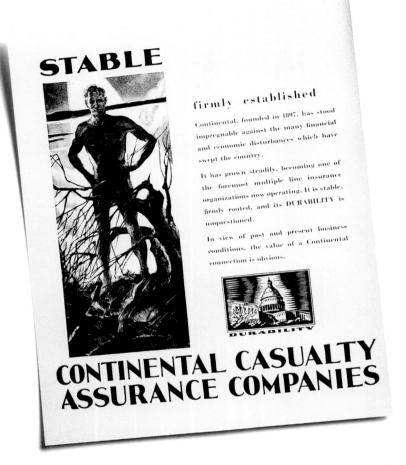

STABLE

firmly established

Continental, founded in 1897, has stood impregnable against the many financial and economic disturbances which have swept the country.

It has grown steadily, becoming one of the foremost multiple line insurance organizations now operating. It is stable, firmly rooted, and its DURABILITY is unquestioned.

In view of past and present business conditions, the value of a Continental connection is obvious.

DURABILITY

CONTINENTAL CASUALTY ASSURANCE COMPANIES

Above
During the 1930s, company advertise-
ments asserted that "Continental
DURABILITY is established BEYOND
questioning," emphasizing its firm
financial foundation, even during the
lean years of the Great Depression.

Opposite page
The first collapse of stock prices on the
New York Stock Exchange was on October
24, 1929. Wealthy investors tried to prop
up the market by buying. Crowds gath-
ered on Wall Street and 400 extra police
officers patrolled the financial district.

The Great Depression and Continental

President Behrens barely had time to settle into his new role when he was confronted by a crisis of international scope. Stock market prices had been declining for weeks and there was panic in the air. Then, on October 29, 1929 — a day forever known as Black Tuesday — investors dumped 16 million shares onto the New York Stock Exchange at declining prices. It was the most catastrophic day in American market history, ushering in the Great Depression.

Within three years, the economy hit rock bottom. By the end of 1932, unemployment peaked at 13 million. Wages declined to 60 percent of their 1929 level. Industry operated at half its 1929 capacity. Businesses reported losses of $6 billion. Agricultural prices spiraled downward. Banks shut their doors. Bedraggled men were standing on America's street corners, with their haunting refrain, "Hey, Buddy, can you spare a dime?"

For the Continental companies, the next few years saw steadily declining business. During this period, executives and employees were forced to reduce their salaries twice, but no employees were laid off.

The Continental companies lost nearly $900,000 in the stock market and their capital and surplus plummeted from $10 million to $7.5 million. Even so, at a time when some insurers were going under, Continental remained solvent. This was due in part to the company having shunned heavy involvement in the mort-gage insurance market, thereby avoiding the home loan defaults which caused other companies to go under. And, since the Continental companies had been prudent enough to invest in fixed income securities like bonds and guaranteed stocks, they were able to use some of those reserves to cover emergencies.

Continental Agents' Record

September
1932

Continental Assurance was able to maintain customer confidence during those bleak years. One way was by allowing customers to cash in their life insurance policies on demand. Continental Assurance withdrew cash from the bank early on in the crisis and stored the money in a company vault. Although legislation allowed insurance companies to withhold payments for 60 days, and limited the amount payable to $100, Continental issued checks for the full amount whenever requested. In many cases, when customers found out they could "cash in" on demand, their trust in the company was maintained and they left the cash right where it was.

With salaries in decline nationwide, Continental Casualty decided to offer a new, inexpensive personal accident policy called "The Ace in the Hole." This policy offered both general liability and auto property damage insurance for a premium ranging from one to three dollars per month. "The Ace in the Hole," the company's first one-policy contract for combined auto liability and property damage, was the most liberal and least expensive on the market.

Continental also became a pioneer in the field of retirement income annuities for people aged 65 and older. The move came before Social Security was created and met a strong public demand for some form of guaranteed retirement income. Naturally, during the trying times of the Depression, long-term security was on most customers' minds.

As the Depression began to wane, President Behrens told stockholders, "We're going ahead in '34." That year, the Continental companies had 10,000 agents in the field with income topping $20 million — a return to the pre-crash levels of 1927. The American economy was on the mend, and so were the Continental companies.

Left and above
Amidst the poverty and scarcity of the Great Depression, the valiant American spirit refused to be broken. Instead the nation found comfort in sports, in the glamour and fantasy of Hollywood movies, and in the swinging sounds of the Big Bands.

1936

Some of the top agents celebrated the 25th anniversary of the Continental Assurance Company at the Edgewater Beach Hotel in Chicago, September 17, 1936.

The rebound continued through the remaining years of the decade. In 1937, Continental ranked as the nation's eighth most successful stock casualty company, with net premium reaching $20 million. A few years later, income was approaching the $40 million mark.

Building the Life Company

The year 1937 saw another changing of the guard. Herman Behrens was elevated to the chairmanship of Continental Casualty and Continental Assurance Companies while remaining president of Continental Assurance. Martin P. Cornelius succeeded Behrens as president of Continental Casualty.

Behrens' goal was to build Continental Assurance, the life company, into as powerful a force as the casualty company. His presidency marked the first time that Continental Assurance had its own chief executive: previously the two companies had been directed by one president.

Continental Assurance's Group Life Department, established in 1930, had become a major profit center. Behrens launched a number of initiatives, including participating insurance — a form of whole life insurance — and pension plans linked to life policies. His strategy paid off. By 1948, Continental Assurance had more than $1 billion in premium.

On the casualty side, to stay competitive in the lucrative market for burglary insurance, Martin Cornelius created a new subsidiary, the Transportation Insurance Company, in 1938. Continental had been unable to offer burglary protection for inland marine activity under its charter. The new company offered lines of inland marine coverage, insuring all perils of transportation including fire, weather, thievery, collision, flood and water damage, and acts of God.

CAC's souvenir program from its Pyramid Club Convention in 1948 marking "A Billion in Force" for its life business.

1911

Our First Billion

CNA/Insurance
Library

1948

The War Years

For America, World War II began on December 7, 1941 — the day that lives in infamy. As the nation went to war, 422 Continental men and women enlisted to fight. Five of the men never returned.

No one at Continental was spared loss during those desperate years: death touched even the highest ranks in the company. In September 1944, Lt. Harry Cornelius, the son of Martin Cornelius — by then general counsel — died of wounds sustained in the battle for Brest on the Atlantic coast of France. Cornelius was only 25.

Opposite page
This American Red Cross enlistment poster appealed to women's sense of patriotic duty. If men could serve, women could also.

This page
Lt. Harry Cornelius, son of Martin Cornelius, died in action during World War II.

Continental's female employees founded their own Red Cross Unit during World War II. It was one of the most active in Chicago.

CONTINENTAL CASUALTY - ASSURANCE COMPANIES PRODUCTION UNIT, CHICAGO CHAPTER, AME
JULY, 1942

RED CROSS

Kaufmann & Fabry
42-2418

At home, Continental agents and employees joined the war effort with a vengeance. They launched programs to buy government bonds, and helped other companies set up payroll deduction systems to fund America's fighting men. Women organized a new chapter of the Red Cross, The Continental Red Cross. Midway through the war, the in-house newsletter, *Family Circle,* reported, "Continental employees have already spoken their piece against bondage with $232,418 invested in war bonds."

As in other industries, as the men went overseas to fight, women began to play an increasingly prominent role in the work force. Continental trained women as underwriters for the first time. The railroad claims department also extended a welcome to women. In 1943, *Family Circle* reported, "We've finally done it! Claims Adjuster Betty McGillivray has the honor of being the first woman to work in the Railroad Department!" And, once women made the breakthrough, they were there to stay.

FDR's "Four Freedoms" are 1) freedom of speech and expression, 2) freedom of worship, 3) freedom from want and 4) freedom from fear. He set them forth in his January 6, 1941 State of the Union address. (Almanac of American History, Schlesinger, Jr., ed., pg. 482)

This Continental advertising campaign borrowed from Franklin D. Roosevelt's famous "Four Freedoms" speech, in which FDR reassured Americans of their right to freedom from want.

On the insurance front, a triumvirate of Continental power players was guiding the companies — Behrens, Cornelius and First Vice President Roy Tuchbreiter, a man who would rise to head both companies upon Behrens' untimely death in 1945. The three decided to turn the Continental companies into the "Department Store of Insurance."

Their first step was to add another "H" to A&H — Hospitalization — and to create a separate division to service the new business. At first, hospitalization policies were limited, mainly attached as riders to accident and disability policies. But the policies quickly expanded to include voluntary accident, sickness, hospital and surgical benefits for wage earners and their dependents. Even the previously uninsurable were covered. People between the ages of 60 and 80 became eligible for benefits that included three, four or five dollars per day toward the cost of a hospital room. The company also agreed to cover congenital diseases and polio.

In moves designed to strengthen and consolidate their gains, the Continental companies launched several initiatives. A campaign to increase policy renewals offered agents a full commission for each renewed policy. Continental also moved into the reinsurance business in order to increase underwriting profits. One of the first deals was reinsurance of all of the outstanding accident, health and hospitalization policies of Franklin Life. Once again, the aggressive strategies paid off: assets topped $54 million in 1943, making it Continental Casualty's biggest year.

Left
Roy Tuchbreiter, born on Chicago's West Side and fatherless at an early age, was a self-made man. He became president of Continental Casualty in 1944 and Continental Assurance in 1945.

Above
Accident and hospitalization insurance brochures often showed loved ones in the hospital.

1944

Continental Casualty Company's 1944 Commercial Accident and Health Conference dinner was held at the Hotel New Yorker.

ASUALTY COMPANY

AND HEALTH CONFERENCE

ER   NEW YORK

RY 25, 1944

You Name It And We'll Insure It

In 1945, with Tuchbreiter as president of both the Continental Casualty and Continental Assurance Companies, Continental Casualty's Special Risks Division was born, and quickly became known as Lloyd's of Chicago. Among the more colorful high-risk policies were

Coverage of all 34 Chicago White Sox under Continental's Special Risk accident protection. The amount of coverage ranged from $10,000 to $50,000 depending on the value of the player's contract.

Coverage of the Little League with a tailor-made accident and injury policy.

Coverage of the Indy 500 drivers, pit crews and officials. The coverage paid off for one driver in 1949, when Duke Nalons' car hit a retaining wall at 126 m.p.h. and burst into flames. Duke was seriously injured but, fortunately, was fully covered by Continental.

Upper right
Continental has been a major insurer of our country's cultural and sports activities since the 1940s, including the boys and girls of Little League.

Lower right
Continental signed up the Chicago White Sox with accident protection beginning in 1945. Long before Edwin Forkel became CCC president in 1959, his college record earned him a tryout with the Chicago White Sox. Forkel chose a career in the insurance industry over a promising career on the baseball field.

Below
Continental has been insuring the race car drivers of the famous Indy 500 since 1948.

Still Flying High

At noon on August 12, 1949, a DC-4 military transport plane gunned its motors and took off from O'Hare Airport, bound for Europe. Riding on its wings was $641,000 in Continental coverage. Aboard the flight were radio star Tommy Bartlett and his troupe of 24 actors, entertainers and technicians setting off on a tour of military bases. It was one of the largest groups of policies the company had ever issued for a single flight.

During the war, Continental Casualty had become the first American firm to write aviation insurance on an all-risk, world-wide basis. Its personal accident policies were so attractive that the United States government selected Continental's new Aviation Accident and Travel Division to protect American troops engaged in air operations both during the war and afterward.

The Aviation Accident and Travel Division was a great success. In 1949, Continental Casualty created the first individual accident policy to cover travel on commercial airliners. The Aviation and Travel Division also took the company in search of *King Solomon's Mines*. Continental insured film stars Deborah Kerr, Stewart Granger, and their production crew during the making of MGM's African epic. An employee newsletter reported, "Mosquitoes and tsetse flies swarmed and stung, a herd of rogue elephants and a rhino charged the safari, lions inspected the camp's garbage at night and snakes spit venom from behind trees."

By 1950, the Special Risks Division was covering 40 White House correspondents on their travels with President Truman. Also that year, the world's foremost archer, Howard Hill, insured his tour of Africa with a $50,000 policy that covered Hill on a seven-month safari into the wilds of the Belgian Congo as he attempted to bring down an elephant with bow and arrow.

Continental designed aviation insurance that covered the risks encountered by airplane travelers, pilots and stewardesses and student pilots.

The elegance of the Beehive Building graces downtown Chicago. Located at 310 South Michigan Avenue, it was the fourth home of CNA (1943-1961). Its nickname derives from the freestanding sculpture of a beehive atop the building, symbolizing industriousness and thrift.

1964

The Fabulous Fifties

In the short span of time from 1950 to 1965, the American economy dazzled the world by producing goods and services at a spectacular rate. It produced nearly as much in that period as it had since the founding of Jamestown in 1607. The economic growth helped sustain the American dream — an idyllic home in the suburbs, a loving family, and a good job. More Americans could strive for the dream since more people were graduating from college than ever before, thanks to the Government Issue (GI) Bill, which awarded education allowances to World War II and Korean War veterans.

The Continental Choraliers, the company's choir created in 1952, was open to any employee who would subscribe to the motto: "There's no fun without music, and no music without fun." Both co-workers and Chicagoans were entertained by the Choraliers as they put on performances around the city, traveling to such places as the Insurance Exchange and Borg-Warner buildings in the Chicago Loop.

With the post-war boom came new forms of leisure and popular culture. Americans were on the move! The new interstate highway system helped create and maintain a mobile culture of motels and fast-food establishments. The baby boom reached its peak and a new demographic phenomenon — teenagers — were shaking their hips to an exciting new style of music called Rock and Roll. Glowing black and white televisions were bringing comedy and drama into America's living rooms. That no one could enjoy the American dream without the protection of insurance was the message being spread in the media by the Continental insurance companies through their innovative advertising campaigns.

However, there was a dark side to the post-war prosperity. The United States had emerged from World War II as a superpower, but it seemed locked in a life-or-death struggle with the Soviet Union — the Cold War. Great Britain's eminent prime minister, Winston Churchill, captured the mood of the time when he declared after the end of World War II that "an iron curtain had descended across Europe." In the 1950s, the United States also became embroiled in the Korean War.

The presidential election of 1952 proved to be pivotal for the United States. For two decades, Democrats had held the White House. In 1952, the Republicans claimed victory when the immensely popular former general Dwight Eisenhower defeated the Democratic contender, Adlai Stevenson, governor of Illinois. Continental played it down the middle by providing both candidates with accident policies for their campaign trips.

CNA employees applied the same enthusiasm to company-organized recreational activities as they did to their work.

Continental employees raised money for the Chicago Community Fund by holding "Bring Your Own Lunch Day" in October 1952. Bringing lunch from home, 2,400 employees donated their lunch money to the Fund.

This gesture on CNA's part was the start of CNA's desire to give back to the community not just in its home territory but nationally as well. Today, the CNA Foundation contributes to charitable organizations across the country as part of its philanthropic efforts.

Miss Contact/Miss Triad

In 1957, Continental created a new magazine called *Contact* to serve as a means of communication among Continental employees. One of the regular features of the monthly magazine was "Miss Contact," a company-wide contest in which winners were pictured on the back cover. Monthly winners were selected from submitted photographs, which were judged by a Chicago advertising agency "for interest and clarity as well as for the beauty of the woman." Annually, employees would choose one of the 12 winners as Miss Contact of the year. By 1963, the contest evolved into Miss Triad, when the *Triad* succeeded *Contact* as the employee news magazine. Times were changing, however. By the publication of the February 1964 issue of the *Triad* — a special issue focusing on career women in insurance — the contest was no longer featured.

AUGUST'S

MISS TRIAD

SHARON SULLIVAN

Visions of orange blossoms are dancing in the pretty, blonde head of this month's Miss TRIAD, Sharon Sullivan from National Fire, here shown taking a tour of the CN Summer Art Festival. Sharon is busy taking care of last-minute details for her wedding on August 24, when she will become Mrs. Danny Gallichio.

Sharon, a petite, 5' 2", 102 pounds, already has a jump on most young brides. She's learned how to keep house and cook by helping her mother, Ollie, who also works at NF in the mail room. "Now I'll have to learn to make Italian spaghetti," Sharon laughs, "but I'll never be able to make Italian dishes the way my fiancee's mother does."

Although busy with last-minute wedding plans and getting their apartment ready, Sharon and her fiancee still find time to take in some favorite sports—dancing, miniature golf and bowling.

Twenty-year old Sharon has been working at National Fire for three years. A bookkeeper in the NF GAO Agency Bookkeeping Department, she started shortly after her graduation from high school.

To this month's lovely Miss TRIAD and her husband-to-be, we add our best wishes.

Applications for the MISS TRIAD contest may be submitted by co-workers or by the girls themselves. Any employee of the Continental National Insurance Group, single or married, may enter. Send a photograph to THE TRIAD. A girl may enter as often as she wishes, but winners may not re-enter. Chicagoans call Extension 5171. Branch personnel contact your TRIAD reporter (see page 3 for listing).
PRINTED IN U.S.A.

Hondorp Mutual

CNA was one of the first insurance companies in the United States to market retirement annuities. The spark was World War II.

The war years were a time of scarcity, as industry turned from producing consumer goods to manufacturing weaponry. With the demand for products (from sugar to shoes) outweighing supplies, prices spiraled upward. In a move to curb runaway inflation, the federal government froze wages.

Employees nationwide were upset and demanded some form of compensation to make up for their loss in real income. CNA's solution was retirement annuities.

Peter Hondorp, who founded and directed CNA's Pension Department in the early 1940s, anticipated that many employers would appease their disgruntled workers by providing pension plans in lieu of pay raises. Group pension plans quickly became an excellent product for CNA.

By 1950, CNA's pensions covered more than 30,000 people and brought in more than $100 million in premium. By 1986, CNA's Pension Department was managing $2.8 billion in assets. Today, its assets total $7 billion.

Glenn Mateja, who worked in the Pension Department from 1969 to 1992, recalled: "As a result of Peter Hondorp's great success with the Pension Department, CNA employees nicknamed the department 'Hondorp Mutual.' Peter Hondorp's foresight and aggressive marketing of annuities catapulted the department into the field of financial services long before most insurance companies."

The Independent Agent

Profound changes marked the insurance industry in the 1950s and affected the Continental insurance companies. Continental Casualty had become America's number one accident and sickness insurance company. But it faced a new challenge, the rise of other insurance companies, such as State Farm, which employed salaried agents to sell policies to customers rather than selling their insurance through independent agencies.

Some companies bowed to the competition from the direct writers and abandoned their system of independent agencies. But Continental's president, Roy Tuchbreiter, identified himself first and foremost as an "agency man." This was the term used at the time to refer to insurance executives, such as Tuchbreiter, who were strongly committed to using and protecting the national network of independent insurance agents. Tuchbreiter chose to rely upon Continental's greatest strength — its strong, dedicated force of independent agents. "Continental is a company that is committed," he wrote, "to the American Agency System of merchandising." Commissions, he believed, motivated agents not only to sell insurance, but to service the customer in an unbeatable way.

Tuchbreiter knew that it was important to give customers efficient and complete service as well as to give agents immediate access to information and technical support. Agents reported directly to the home office or to one of the company branch offices scattered throughout the country. Branch offices in the 1950s were of three general types: multiple lines, accident and health (A&H), and claims. Small branches like New Haven employed one or two people at most, while large offices like New York employed well over 400. Each branch office and each division was responsible for its own budget and bottom line. Both branch managers and agents were encouraged to design and execute their own business strategies.

"The big thing to get ahead is to know and understand both

yourself and people, add to that plenty of hard work."

— Roy Tuchbreiter

Leadership for the 1950s

With Continental's branch offices now dotting the nation, President Tuchbreiter aligned himself with other strong agency men such as J.M. "Mil" Smith, who became Continental Casualty's first vice president of A&H in 1951, and Howard Reeder at Continental Assurance, who was named executive vice president.

Mil Smith was known as a man who combined an ingenious mind with a daring willingness to experiment. Ahead of his time, Smith specialized in spotting market niches and designing products to fit them. He began and ended his career with Continental, and his rise through the ranks possessed a Horatio Alger quality. In a 1957 profile in the business magazine *Success Unlimited*, Smith wrote, "I entered the accident and health underwriting department of Continental Casualty Company in 1925 as assistant to the damn good office boy they already had." Thirty-one years later, Smith capped his career as president of Continental Casualty, being recognized as one of the best merchandisers in the A&H field.

Howard Reeder entered the insurance industry in 1927 as a trained mathematician and experienced actuary. A 10-cigars-and-pipes-a-day smoker, Reeder proved a pioneer in the field of group life insurance. His ideas on insurance demonstrated that he was a forward-looking leader. He once remarked that insurance is "a risk-taking business, which is guided by the law of averages." His keen understanding of averages helped him build Continental Assurance into one of the nation's largest life insurance companies and ensured his climb to the chairmanship.

Howard Reeder, Chairman 1965–1971

Howard Reeder's first attempt at selling life insurance was in high school. He drummed up business for the local agency, headed by his stepfather, earning enough in commission to pay his way through college.

Roy Tuchbreiter (left), Chairman 1956–1965

J.M. "Mil" Smith (right), President 1956–1959
Continental Casualty Company.

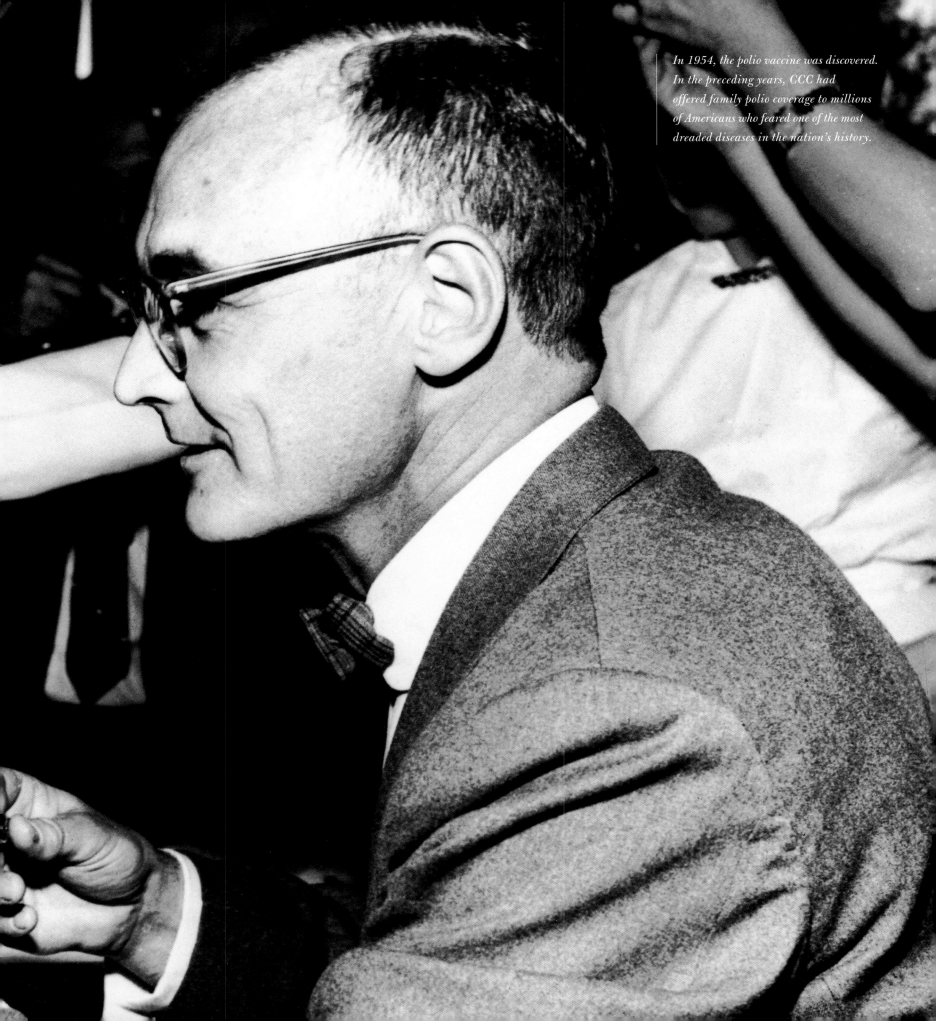

In 1954, the polio vaccine was discovered. In the preceding years, CCC had offered family polio coverage to millions of Americans who feared one of the most dreaded diseases in the nation's history.

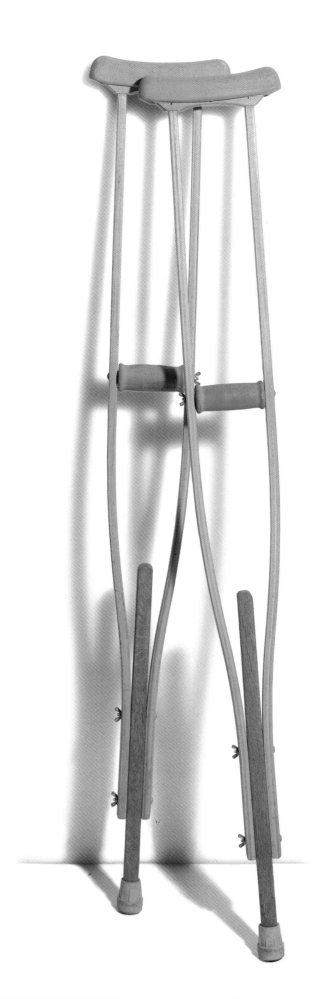

The Polio Policy

Polio was America's most dreaded disease at mid-century, striking high and low, and extending its devastating reach even into the White House. With great dignity, President Franklin D. Roosevelt suffered paralysis caused by polio. Because hospital and medical expenses for severe cases were astronomically high, few companies could afford to offer polio insurance. Those that did provided only limited coverage.

In 1949, Mil Smith began marketing a polio policy that was affordable for entire families. For $10, a family could purchase two years of coverage, providing blanket benefits of $5,000 for each family member. The company expected to sell $1.5 million in premium that first year. Instead, three-quarters of a million people lined up to purchase the Polio Policy — $7.5 million worth! Agents found customers lining up outside their doors and were required to work nights and weekends just to meet the demand. In some cases, underwriting had to be subcontracted. Stock clerks and printers had to work around the clock to keep up with the demand for policy forms and applications.

Ironically, the same year that the Polio Policy was introduced was also the worst year in two decades for polio outbreaks. Some company executives questioned whether or not Continental should continue to offer the policy. But Smith argued on behalf of ethics and the long haul: Continental could not offer coverage one year and then retract it the next when the spread of the disease unexpectedly increased. The company owed it to its customers to stay the course — and it did.

CCC offered free polio policy sales aids to agents, including banners and posters for display, and circulars for distribution to prospects.

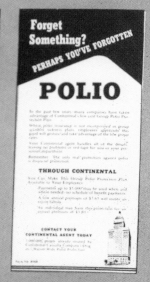

Protect Our Nation's Youth

Continental Casualty has been a major player in our nation's sports and cultural activities. A pioneer in camp insurance since 1945, Continental took its innovative coverage a step further in 1952, when it launched the Protect Our Nation's Youth (PONY) program. PONY policies offered medical expense reimbursement for accidents to children from kindergarten through college. Three major areas were covered: camping activities, student activities and organized sports.

Young athletes around the country were protected by Continental's Sport Program. College students too old to be included on a family policy and not yet covered by an employer's health plan benefited from PONY's Student Program. PONY was present at youth events such as the Boy Scouts' Third Annual National Jamboree, where it insured the 50,000 scouts in attendance and the Jamboree's California headquarters.

Continental's commitment to the safety and well-being of the nation's young people extended beyond insurance. As part of PONY, the company teamed up with the American Camping Association to issue a newsletter that included safety tips for campers and assisted the American College Health Association in a public service project, among other things.

Innovative Products for Changing Times

Mil Smith recognized that senior citizens were an important but under-represented market niche. Continental Casualty originated the concept of selling group health insurance to persons over 65. The New York State Retired Teachers Association was the first group to be covered. The contract proved profitable and CCC began to solicit new business. By 1957, the company noted in its annual report that it was providing hospital-medical-surgical insurance for more than 75,000 members of two important associations of elderly people: the National Retired Teachers Association and the National Association of Retired Civil Employees. During the latter part of that year, the company launched a radical experiment in the State of Iowa involving the offering of hospital-surgical insurance to all of the people in that state aged 65 or over, without evidence of insurability.

Two years later, the company offered the industry's first comprehensive group dental insurance plan. The new products immediately resulted in record increases in net premium of $28.6 million. By 1962, the dental plan was so popular that the American Dental Association signed up its employees.

Professional associations became one of Continental Casualty's most lucrative A&H markets. As one company executive aptly put it, "the reason behind the steadiness of high volume sales seems to be most easily summed up in one word: associations." Beginning in the late 1940s, the company began aggressively targeting national associations. Some of America's most prestigious professional associations have since formed partnerships with CCC, such as the American Medical Association, the American Bar Association, and the American Institute of Architects.

Fire Insurance Sparks Further Growth

By the end of 1951, Continental Casualty ranked third in premium writing among all stock casualty companies in the country. Premium volume reached $115 million, with over $65 million in accident and health business. Continental Assurance ranked 23rd among life insurance companies and would soon reach the $2 billion mark in paid-for life insurance in force.

President Tuchbreiter decided the time was ripe to bring Continental — having become a mature company with more than 50 years' standing — to the next level. Taking advantage of the company's strong financial position, he inaugurated a series of strategic mergers and acquisitions lasting well into the next decade. In 1952, United States Life (U.S. Life) became the first addition to the Continental family of companies. The purchase proved both a sound investment and an impetus to further growth. U.S. Life brought strong foreign operations as well as competitive domestic sales to the deal. The U.S. Life acquisition helped move Continental into a field it had not yet developed, non-participating insurance.

Major changes in state insurance laws sparked Continental's next move. Historically, insurance in the United States had been divided into three basic lines: casualty, fire and life insurance. The changes in state laws beginning with New York in 1949 and reaching all states by 1956, provided that individual companies could now engage in multiple lines of insurance. This allowed Continental to attain a goal set decades before — to become a multiple lines insurer.

Left
In 1948, CAC was the first life insurance company organized under the laws of the State of Illinois to have written $2 billion in life insurance. CAC celebrated by circulating this poster advertising its $2 billion milestone.

1958

The Continental National Insurance Institute (CNII) was opened in 1957, providing college level instruction in five major insurance categories to promising Continental career employees. The Agents' School, offered through CNII, was a personalized program aimed at familiarizing agents with the company's products and advising them as to the latest and most successful sales methods.

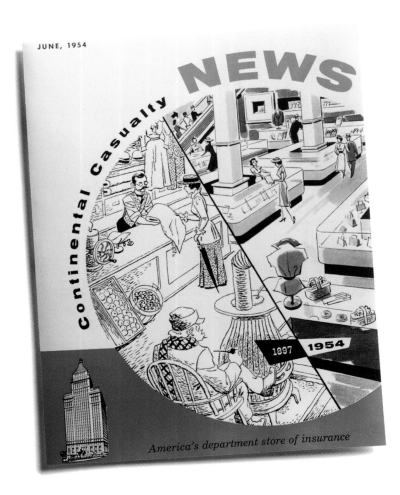

By 1954, Continental advertised itself as a "Department Store of Insurance" because it offered insurance buyers multiple lines of coverage.

Since insurance companies were now permitted to expand into other lines, Continental Casualty immediately created a fire division under George N. Duncan, a 22-year veteran of the fire insurance business. The fire division offered coverages for all types of property, insuring against direct loss by fire, with extended coverage for perils such as windstorm, hail, explosion, riot, damage by aircraft, water damage by sprinkler leakage, and subsequent loss of rental income. During 1954, the company's first year in the field, it wrote $2.5 million in premium.

With the enactment of multiple lines legislation, Continental's Department Store of Insurance could now offer one-stop shopping. The first of the newly combined and newly marketed fire and casualty policies was called a "package" policy, and it was made available to homeowners. For a single premium, the package policy included property coverage for a dwelling and its contents, plus personal liability insurance. Continental developed four package policies, offering a choice of coverage options for homeowners in those early years. By 1956, it was writing $225 million in premium.

By mid-century, the actuarial and accounting functions were under enormous strain, pressured to keep up with the demands of calculating increasingly complex financial data. The days of keeping records on file cards were long past and even the more modern electronic calculating machines were not up to the task. So in 1955, company management decided to turn to "The Brain" — one of the earliest IBM mainframe computers. Putting "The Brain" to work was the responsibility of a full-time team of actuaries and technicians. It took a couple of years to get the computer up and running. In the early IBM days, there were racks and rooms of equipment, miles of punch tape, boxes of punch cards. The next 30 years would see all of it condensed into desktop computers.

*In 1955, company management decided
to turn to "The Brain" — one of the
earliest IBM mainframe computers.*

NATIONAL

Fire Insurance Company,
OF HARTFORD,
CONNECTICUT.

Representing the
NATIONAL
FIRE INSURANCE COMPANY
OF
HARTFORD CONN.

OVER.

The Continental-National Group

In 1956, Continental sold most of its stake in U.S. Life for a profit of $6.8 million. Six months later, Continental courted the National Fire Insurance Company of Hartford, Connecticut, founded in 1869. It was one of the best known names in the insurance industry and, by the mid-1950s, it was annually writing $79 million in premium.

Roy Tuchbreiter announced in December 1956 that Continental had purchased 66.8 percent of the total outstanding stock of National Fire. Thus was born the Continental-National Group (CN Group), consisting of the Continental Casualty Company, the Continental Assurance Company, and the National Fire Insurance Company of Hartford. The new alignment made Continental the third largest multiple lines insurer in the United States, with combined net premium of $415 million. A Continental newsletter for agents promised, "The CN Group will be an ever-increasing power to meet the unique challenges of a new era in the insurance industry."

To meet the goals of the newly formed CN Group, the position of chairmanship was reinstated after an 11-year hiatus. Roy Tuchbreiter, reigning president of both Continental Casualty and Continental Assurance, was the obvious candidate. His move up to the chairmanship left two vacancies. Mil Smith became president of Continental Casualty and Howard Reeder was appointed president of Continental Assurance.

Despite Continental-National's unquestioned strength, 1956 was the beginning of a difficult time for the group. While Continental Assurance had enjoyed a successful year, with nearly $5 billion in life insurance in force, Continental Casualty was posting its first loss since 1935. The accident and health division had shown a profit, but it was undercut by the enormous losses on the property and casualty side. Automobile accidents accounted for the lion's share of these losses, in part due to the escalating claims awarded in the nation's courts. The automobile problem proved to be the first in a series of setbacks that have haunted the insurance industry. At about this time, CNA underwrote a commercial risk for $17,000 in premium for Fibreboard Corporation, a construction materials manufacturer. Years later, in 1993, this assumed risk would prove extremely costly when CNA would pay more than $2 billion as part of an asbestos claims settlement and its related expenses.

The relationship between National Fire Insurance of Hartford and Continental Casualty was forged before their merger in 1956. During the 1930s, National Fire and Continental Casualty worked together to offer multi-peril automobile policies, at a time when single companies were not legally allowed to issue multi-peril policies.

1963

Under the leadership of Dr. Martin Luther King, Jr., 25,000 people participated in a non-violent civil rights march from Selma to Montgomery, Alabama. President Lyndon B. Johnson asked CIC — the company with which CNA would later merge — to write the bond for the railroad company that agreed to stand ready in case the marchers' lives were in danger.

The Rebellious Sixties

On January 3, 1960, Senator John F. Kennedy announced his candidacy for the presidency. The election of this young and vigorous president set the stage for the turbulent decade ahead which would be dominated by the struggle for civil rights in the American South and the war in Vietnam. The number of casualties in Vietnam increased to tens of thousands as American military involvement escalated during the 1960s. At home, anti-war riots broke out as did protests against racial injustice. On college campuses, thousands of young people joined protest movements. It all happened to a beat played by groups with strange names like the Beatles, the Doors and the Grateful Dead. The nation was under stress and strain and so was the insurance industry.

In the 1960s, Continental Casualty's personal property and casualty lines continued to flounder. These lines, primarily homeowners and auto insurance, accounted for 19 percent of Continental's business. Accident and health remained profitable, with 54 percent of the business. Nevertheless, the continued rise in auto-related payouts was cutting into company profits. By 1963, auto claims led to underwriting losses of $14.6 million.

These problems were not Continental's alone. The entire industry was suffering from astronomical settlements awarded by juries, spiraling medical costs, economic inflation and new forms of regulation and legislation that limited rate increases by insurers. Between 1955 and 1970, casualty companies suffered $1.5 billion in underwriting losses. The 14 largest firms alone lost $609 million during the 1960s.

To find solutions for these financial difficulties, the company reorganized its leadership. In 1962, Tuchbreiter remained chairman, but Reeder, still holding the presidency of Continental Assurance, was promoted to the newly created position of co-chairman. One year later, David G. Scott replaced Reeder as president of Continental Assurance. Edwin Forkel, who had replaced Mil Smith in 1959, remained president of Continental Casualty.

Tuchbreiter and Reeder, as co-chairs, came up with a two-part strategy to reinvigorate and reposition the CN Group. First, they decided to redefine underwriting risk and trim personal property and casualty lines. By 1962, those lines were cut back to nine percent of the business. Next, they launched a company-wide consolidation. They realized that the three companies in the group — Continental Casualty, Continental Assurance and National Fire — were duplicating services and products. Reeder, therefore, personally supervised the merger of departments, branches and product lines to drastically reduce unnecessary operating expenses. After the reorganization, claims were handled by a single, integrated department which handled all property and casualty, surety, and excess and surplus policies. The result was a streamlined and efficient operation that was better able to focus on customer service.

In addition, new and profitable products were designed and targeted at specific mass markets. "Golden 65," for example, was a major medical plan aimed at senior citizens. Mass marketing was used again in Canada to launch "Medical," a policy designed to supplement government health programs. Continental then embarked on a campaign called "Protect America's Income," which helped young wage earners by providing them with a guaranteed income in case of disability. In many ways, these innovations were simply more sophisticated versions of earlier Continental policies. Programs like these added millions of dollars to the bottom line.

Top photo
Student protesters at Columbia
University. New York City, 1968.

Bottom photo
Demonstrators calling for peace at home
and in Vietnam. Des Moines, Iowa 1968.

Guaranteed Renewable's new Paid Up At Age 65 Hospitalization Policy gets Warm Reception at Detroit highly successful meeting are standing L to R, Earl Williams, Special Agent; Rick Gilmore, Superinten Division; Bob Martin, Regional Supervisor; Ron Green, Resident Vice-President Detroit Branch; Mike Manager. Kneeling are L to R, Art Donahue, Special Agent; Morris Dudley, Guaranteed Renewable Hoglan, Special Agent; Fred Johnston, Special Agent; Tony Hepp, Guaranteed Renewable Division H said "This was one of the most successful meetings that we have had thus far in our campaign".

WATCH FOR GUARANTEED RENEWABLE'S NEW-PAID UP AT AGE 65 HOSPITALIZATION

Go "On The Town" with Guaranteed Renewable

Attending the
...ranteed Renewable
Detroit A&H Branch
Home Office; Ernie
ce. As Rick Gilmore

! !

Detroit branch agents posed for a celebratory photo after a successful meeting on the Guaranteed Renewable Division's new Paid Up At Age 65 policy.

Continental also offset losses with investment income. During 1963, for example, the company began to shift its portfolio from tax-exempt to taxable securities. Over the course of a year, Continental-National sold $75 million of tax-exempt securities and replaced them with short- and medium-term government and corporate issues. The result was increased income of $1.3 million. In all, the company realized pretax earnings of $30 million in 1964, up sharply from the previous year.

Continental Assurance, meanwhile, was doing quite well in the market and had become one of the nation's fastest-growing, publicly-owned stock life companies. CAC's success was largely due to the innovative products introduced at the time, and a hard-charging sales force. According to Pat O'Neill, the vice president and director of agencies on the East Coast for much of the 1960s and 1970s

CAC was one of the first major life insurance companies to rate term insurance. If you had a medical problem or a family history, a lot of companies would reject your request for term life insurance. But Continental Assurance provided the insurance. We were doing things that other companies would not do back in the 1950s and 1960s.

By fostering *esprit de corps* and introducing good life products, Continental Assurance enjoyed tremendous prestige in the industry.

A&E Program Celebrated 40th Anniversary in 1997

In 1957, CNA, in conjunction with underwriting manager Victor O. Schinnerer & Company, developed the first professional liability insurance program specifically for architects and engineers. CNA and Schinnerer worked closely with the American Institute of Architects and the National Society of Professional Engineers/PEPP in order to understand the liability needs of architects and engineers. Since the program's inception, it has earned the continuous commendation of these highly respected organizations. The Architects and Engineers Liability Program celebrated its 40th anniversary in 1997, CNA's centennial year.

Lloyd's of Chicago

Along with more traditional policies, Continental-National continued to offer the kind of high-risk, high-profile insurance protection that earned it the nickname Lloyd's of Chicago. The creation of the Reinsurance and the Excess and Surplus (E&S) departments in 1954 and 1955 allowed the company to greatly expand its coverages for unusual risks.

On a foggy January day in 1954, for example, Mamie Eisenhower, wife of the general and president, cracked a champagne bottle across the bow of America's first atomic submarine, the U.S.S. Nautilus, inaugurating a new era in naval history. Continental provided accident coverage for the testing of the sub through its Aviation and Travel Accident Division. That was not the company's only foray into the early atomic age. When the Coast Guard launched the world's first nuclear buoy in Chesapeake Bay, Continental Casualty backed the project with a public liability policy covering radiation exposure.

Surety was also active and expanding. One of the largest surety bonds to have been written was executed by Continental Casualty for construction of the Hungry Horse Dam in Montana. For a premium of $460,000, Continental provided surety bonds for bid, performance and payment totaling $9,500,000. When President Truman threw the switch at the opening of the dam in October of 1952, Continental's participation in the massive project had increased the company's visibility and standing in the surety market.

One brilliant sunny day in the early 1960s, the Navy's famed Blue Angels precision flight team looped, dipped and dived over downtown Chicago. It was all in a day's work for the pilots and for the E&S and Reinsurance Departments, which underwrote a $1 million spectator liability policy, with combined bodily injury and property damage coverage.

Top
In 1954 Mamie Eisenhower smashed a champagne bottle against the bow of the U.S.S. Nautilus.

Bottom
The Blue Angels.

153

1961

John F. Kennedy and Jacqueline Bouvier Kennedy, 1961.

At age 43, John F. Kennedy became the youngest man in American history to be elected president. At his inauguration, Kennedy advised, "Ask not what your country can do for you; ask what you can do for your country."

The company wrote two policies for the inauguration activities of President John F. Kennedy in 1961. One was a public liability policy with a $5 million cap. It covered participants in all the inaugural activities, including the parade, the ball, the cloak rooms, and the mailing of tickets and medals. Despite one of the worst snow storms in Washington, D.C.'s history, there was only one claim: an inauguration committee member filed a reimbursement claim after snagging his pants on a board left sticking out by a carpenter at the corner of Pennsylvania Avenue and 14th Street.

In 1965, Ed Sullivan Productions signed a special reinsurance policy for The Beatles concert at Shea Stadium. The policy covered any out-of-pocket expenses due to cancellation or postponement of the historic concert caused by inclement weather. In fact, for decades the company has been heavily involved in entertainment insurance providing non-appearance coverage, workers' compensation, and stop-production policies. Performers and productions covered by CNA have ranged from the famous actress, Rosalind Russell, in her 1958 Broadway hit, "Auntie Mame," to recent sensations like "Cats" and movie blockbusters such as "Batman."

In 1968, the company wrote liability insurance for the Democratic Convention in Chicago. When tear gas canisters began to fly and demonstrators launched a running battle with police, Continental paid millions of dollars for damage to buildings and interruptions caused at the convention.

Continental participated in insuring an early theater-televised boxing match. As Sonny Liston and Floyd Patterson duked it out for the first time, Continental was one of the insurers protecting the sponsors from potential losses caused by a breakdown of the television transmission to theaters across the country.

Opposite page
The Beatles concert at Shea Stadium in New York.

Below
The Sonny Liston and Floyd Patterson boxing match at Comiskey Park, Chicago in 1962.

Continental has insured America's space program since its inception. In the late 1950s, for example, the company insured the seven men who were stationed around the globe to monitor the early, unmanned moon probes. When Apollo 16 went to the moon in 1972, Continental covered the astronauts John Young, Thomas Mattingly and Charles Duke with a $50,000 accidental death policy from the moment they entered the capsule through splashdown recovery.

In addition to insuring the famous, the company offered transportation coverage to the unusual and unknown, such as two traveling baby orangutans owned by the Toledo Zoo. Their agent remarked, "It was just like insuring a person."

Also insured was an unhappy architect who designed a bowling alley with lanes that were six feet too short! The entire end of the building had to be rebuilt at a cost of $21,000. Fortunately, he was covered with an Architects & Engineers Professional Liability contract.

Architects and Engineers coverage has proven to be a profitable line of business for Continental since 1957. Among the outstanding feats of construction covered by the company are the St. Louis Centennial Arch, designed by the noted Finnish architect, Eero Saarinen, and the I.M. Pei-designed East Wing of the National Gallery of Art in Washington, D.C.

The Apollo 16 Saturn V space vehicle, 1972.

In 1962, the CNA Center was completed in Chicago. The company's new sleek 22-story headquarters cost $18 million and was the first skyscraper in the city to feature exposed structural steel as a design element. The building won high praise from architects and city planners for its extensive use of special tinted glass, but the most striking feature of the building's appearance was the contrast of stainless steel window frames against the black paint of the steel columns and beams. The building was subsequently painted red when the south CNA office tower was constructed in 1972. The South tower, which is 44 stories tall, became known as "Big Red." Today, the entire complex is referred to as CNA Plaza.

The CNA Group consisted of the
following eight companies:

Continental Casualty Company

Transportation Insurance Company,
a subsidiary of Continental Casualty

Continental Assurance Company

National Fire Insurance Company
of Hartford

Transcontinental Insurance Company,
a subsidiary of National Fire

American Casualty Company

Valley Forge Insurance Company,
a subsidiary of American Casualty

Valley Forge Life Company,
a subsidiary of American Casualty

Putting the "A" in CNA

The Continental-National Group made a major acquisition on October 28, 1963 — one that put the "A" in CNA. In a $40 million stock transaction, Continental-National acquired the American Casualty Company of Reading, Pennsylvania, the third largest fire and casualty stock company in the United States, with a combined premium volume of $546.8 million. Chairman Tuchbreiter wrote, "In view of the great importance attached to this acquisition for the Continental-National Group, we have changed our name to the Continental-National American Group." In time, that unwieldy name was shortened to the now familiar CNA.

American Casualty's financial situation had been disappointing in the years leading to the takeover. However, CN Group gained a number of advantages from the acquisition, including wider agency representation, greater diversification of risks, greater underwriting capacity, and better service to its policyholders.

In 1964, a year of consolidation and realignment, CNA's growth in premium volume was excellent, showing an increase in net writings of nearly 10 percent to more than $600 million. Continental Assurance alone accounted for $1 billion in assets, becoming the first Illinois life company to join that exclusive business circle. In the same pioneering spirit, CNA was responsible for the 1965 debut of a new insurance product: long term care. This established the leadership position that CNA LTC still holds today.

The creation of the CNA Group was Roy Tuchbreiter's final legacy to the company he had joined 50 years previously. When he reached mandatory retirement age in 1965, Tuchbreiter stepped aside, and Howard Reeder — who had been sharing the chairmanship since 1962 — took over the office. In a farewell message to his employees, Tuchbreiter observed

"Nobody gets to the top rung of the ladder without having somebody hold the ladder. You don't make something of people. You give them an opportunity to make something of themselves."

1997

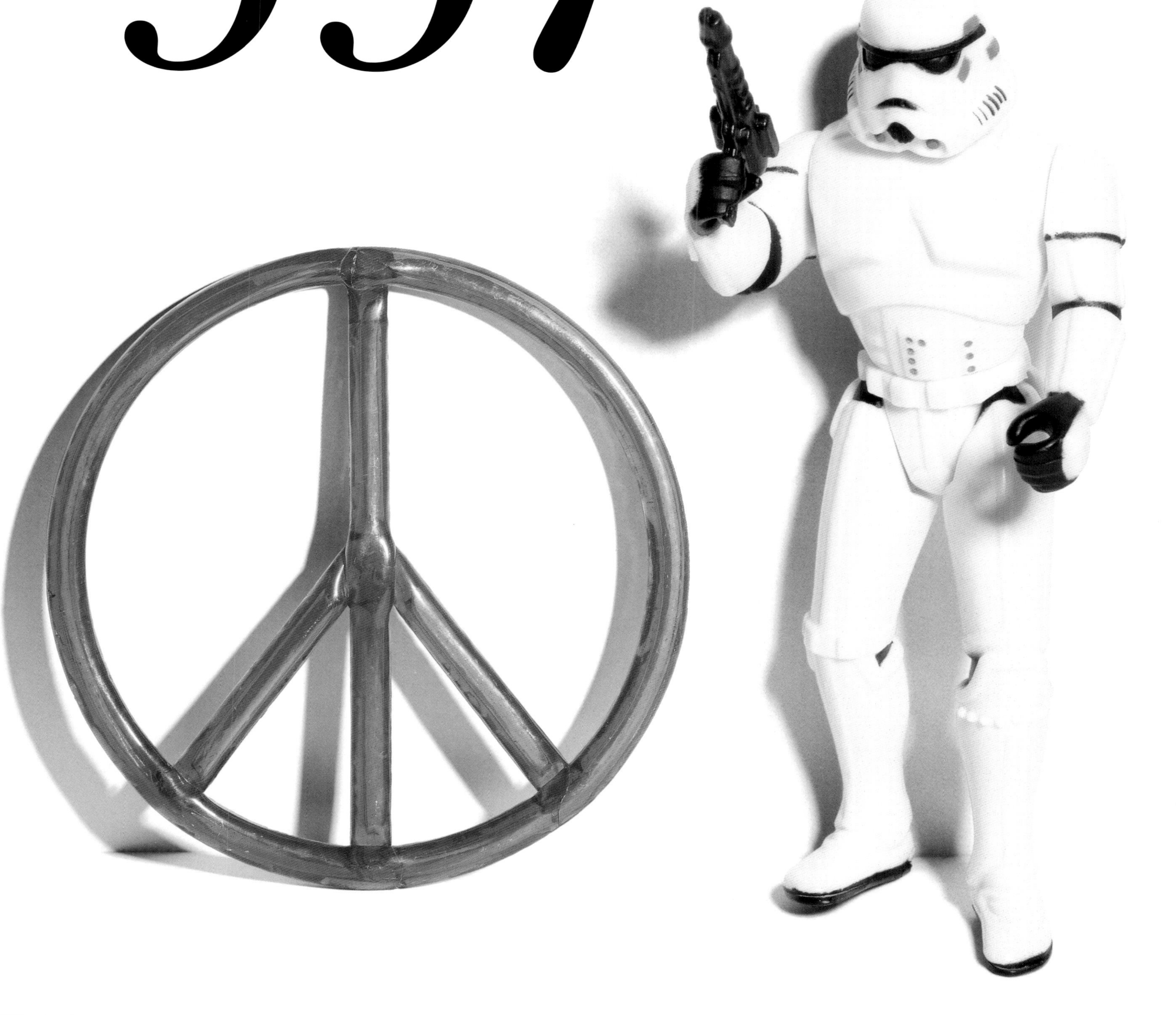

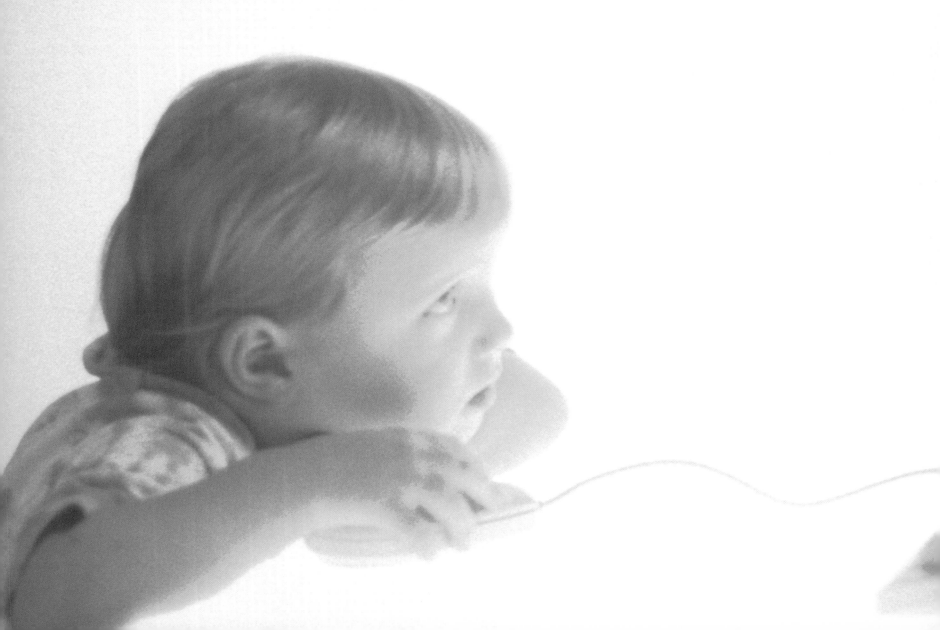

A New Vision for the Company:
Diversification Into Non-insurance Ventures

Howard Reeder took charge of CNA in 1965 after the retirement of Roy Tuchbreiter. Having joined the company in 1941 as vice president and actuary, Reeder was elected a director of Continental Assurance that same year and became executive vice president in 1947. It was under Reeder's leadership that Continental Assurance pioneered group pension plans and group discounts. In 1956, he was named president of Continental Assurance, where he remained until he became co-chairman with Tuchbreiter of the Continental National Group in 1962.

As chairman, Reeder immediately set forth a new direction and a new vision for the company. He called his vision "synerance"— a combination of synergy and insurance. *Finance Magazine* reported that Reeder's goal was "... to equip our sales force as well as to sell full financial security to families." Reeder saw few, if any, limits to CNA's growth, stressing that insurance would continue to be the bedrock of the company. He further noted that mutual funds and consumer finance were high on his wish list as well.

Catching the expansive spirit of the times, Reeder began to move the company in an entirely new direction. On December 31, 1967, a holding company called the CNA Financial Corporation (CNAF) was created to prepare for diversification. Jim MacGinnitie, then head of planning and development for CNAF, recalled "The mood was one of excitement. At the same time, there was some concern that management would forget that the insurance operations were the bread and butter of the company." One company executive was quick to point out that CNAF was a Capricorn. "I may as well add that some thoughtful person in our own organization," he wrote, "has already had a company horoscope prepared — cast by computer, of course — and it says that CNA is warm, friendly, dynamic, has a good head for finance, and is likely to find happiness in marriage."

Reeder had hard-nosed reasons for the move toward diversification. He told *The Wall Street Journal*, "We had more than $200 million of surplus we didn't think we needed for our insurance business, and we were concerned that some raider would take us over if we didn't diversify to make anti-trust and size problems for them."

In 1967 with the battle cry, "We make money work!" CNA Financial made the first of many acquisitions. The diversification strategy paid quick dividends. The stock doubled between 1968 and 1969, the first year it traded on the New York Stock Exchange. However, CNA was about to enter the most difficult period in its history.

One of CNA's core values — financial strength — was predicted as part of its company horoscope in the 1960s. Today, CNA continues to be financially strong.

CNA FINANCIAL CORPORATION

CONSOLIDATED BALANCE SHEET

	December 31	
	1967	1966*
ASSETS		
Cash	$ 57,769,543	$ 66,395,117
Bonds	1,127,430,407	1,081,698,518
Stocks:		
Preferred	106,776,872	85,509,156
Common	477,408,496	384,044,199
Mortgage loans	455,464,113	409,664,106
Policy loans	85,053,439	75,096,689
Real estate	31,626,580	30,476,871
Administrative office buildings	41,702,709	40,803,879
Insurance premiums in course of collection	116,340,741	105,653,521
...nce expense, net of provision for income tax	40,345,945	41,866,263
	20,149,027	18,430,144
	45,777,460	34,452,247
	$2,605,845,335	$2,374,090,714

$ 887,301,5
228,357,

In 1977, PACER celebrated its 10th anniversary. Bill Wiest is pictured center in the first row.

PACER: A Premier Agency Council

Since 1924 life agents have had an ongoing dialogue with CNA through GAMA, the General Agents and Managers Association. In 1967, it was the property and casualty agents' turn to find their voice.

Under the leadership of Bill Wiest, Philadelphia's branch manager, CNA established an advisory council called PACER — The Professional Agents' Council, Eastern Region. PACER was designed as an open and honest forum in which agents and senior managers of CNA could meet annually to discuss common problems and suggest solutions.

Wiest recalled, "We [the Eastern Region and Philadelphia branch] were having service and market problems. We thought that it would be a good idea to get a group of agents together to discuss our problems."

The first meeting (which included CNA executives) at the Reading Motor Inn on May 8, 1967 got off to a rocky start. Wiest recalled that the agents weren't willing to speak up. The CNA executives took charge. Wiest knew that the roles needed to be reversed if PACER was to succeed.

During the next meeting, Wiest asked CNA's executives to leave the room for a few minutes. Wiest then turned to the agents and declared: "You guys are not doing your job. It's your meeting. Don't let the company people run it." CNA's managers must have been surprised when they came back into the room. The agents, Wiest remembered, "took over and they loved it." According to Wiest, from then on the agents "ran the meetings, and they pointed out the various problems with the company — marketing, production and underwriting problems. Senior vice presidents were there. Each guy [vice president] reported back to the chairman. At PACER, there was a terrific two-way communication, and the agents said it was the only group like this in the industry."

This forum of ideas has proven to be an excellent sounding board for CNA, leading to development of new products and better service. PACER has played a vital role in CNA's success. As CNA celebrated its 100th year in 1997, PACER celebrated 30 years as CNA's property and casualty agency council.

Losses Mount

One of CNA's most visible problems proved to be a well-known mutual funds company, the Tsai Management & Research Corporation, which it had purchased in August 1968 for stock valued at almost $32 million. The acquisition brought founder Gerald Tsai, Jr. into CNA as executive vice president in charge of non-insurance acquisitions. He also oversaw CNA's investment portfolio. Tsai was one of the hottest stock pickers of the 1960s, but his golden touch seemed to desert him soon after he joined the company. His Manhattan Fund, worth $381 million in 1968, soon sank and became one of the country's worst-performing mutual funds by 1970.

CNA's other purchases didn't do much better. The home-building firm, the Larwin Group, was purchased by CNA in 1969 for $150 million. Larwin had to be written off at a loss of more than $124 million in 1974 when the housing market turned sour. CNA Nuclear Leasing proved marginally profitable, but tied up $200 million in credit capacity. Another new venture, CNA Realty, posted heavy losses from holdings of real estate equity investments, ranging from dormitories to hotels.

First row from left:
Howard C. Reeder, Chairman of the Board
and President
Gerald Tsai, Executive Vice President

Second row from left:
David G. Scott, Executive Vice President
John A. Henry, Vice President
Boyd N. Everett, Senior Financial Vice President
Paul H. Brown, Vice President
Jacque W. Sammet, Vice President

The Bedrock Starts to Crumble

Exacerbating CNA's problems, the insurance business was failing. Between 1967 and 1970, Reeder's team was stretched by the number and variety of new acquisitions, leaving the core companies, CCC and CAC, without adequate oversight.

In addition, the company had been hurt by major structural problems for some time. Phil Engel, current president of CNA, recalled

There was nothing in common between the Continental Assurance and the Continental Casualty Companies. We were in the same building, but we had different furniture standards, different people, different automation ... nothing came together until we got up to the board level.

To further complicate the situation, the life and casualty companies were competing for the health insurance business. As Engel put it, "The insurance companies were at each other's throats."

As a result, in addition to creating CNAF, Reeder launched a series of initiatives aimed at improving the insurance operations. In 1969, an operating group called Combined Operations — joining together health, reinsurance and international — was set up to develop uniform sales methods. Walter Foody was made senior vice president of CCC and CAC and head of Combined Operations. Herbert DePrenger was named executive vice president of CAC and George McDonnell was appointed executive vice president of CCC. Meanwhile, CNA's insurance operations were placed under the direction of Jacque Sammet, president, CCC and CAC.

Left to right
Walter M. Foody, Jacque W. Sammet,
Herbert L. DePrenger and George F. McDonnell

1965 *Hurricane Betsy caused losses unparalleled in insurance history. New Orleans and the surrounding areas were the hardest hit, with officials declaring that not a single structure had escaped some sort of damage.*

Project 70's purpose was to make the Liability, Property and Surety Division self-sufficient by 1970. Monthly reminders were distributed to employees, emblazoned with the Project 70 logo.

Even as CNA's management team grappled with organizational problems, it continued to be plagued by losses in personal lines, particularly private passenger auto, which had been unprofitable for more than a decade. Other lines were posting operating losses as well. 1965 was also an exceptionally bad year for catastrophic wind losses. When Hurricane Betsy roared through Louisiana and Mississippi, it left a trail of destruction, culminating in the largest catastrophic loss in the history of the insurance industry. Betsy alone produced a gross loss for CNA in excess of $10 million. After reinsurance recoveries, the CNA Group still had a wind damage net loss of $2.5 million, a significant portion of CNA's 1965 underwriting loss of $35 million.

Late in 1967, Reeder summoned his top executives to an emergency session to discuss the mounting problems with the property and casualty lines. One suggestion was to scrap the Liability, Property and Surety Division altogether. That idea was rejected but the meeting resulted in an important plan called Project 70, which led to a number of far-reaching changes in the way the CNA Group did business.

Project 70 was designed to be the driving force toward improving the bottom line in liability, property and surety. The plan placed a new emphasis on procuring large commercial insurance accounts and was marked by an aggressive effort to sign up Fortune 500 companies such as Martin Marietta (now Lockheed Martin). The new focus was further reinforced when agents' commissions on fire and personal auto lines were cut five percent.

By 1970, the Liability, Property and Surety Division was beginning to turn around. Net written premium had increased to $388 million with more than 65 percent of it in commercial lines, and a break-even combined ratio was achieved.

Reeder Steps Down

Even as Project 70 was declared a success for the insurance operations, losses continued to mount at CNAF. In 1971, Reeder reached mandatory retirement age and stepped down. The chief contender for the top position was David G. Scott, by then CNAF's executive vice president. However, the board preferred someone who wasn't so closely associated with the strategies of the past.

For the first time in the company's history, the board of directors decided to reach outside for a new chairman. The choice was not easy. With the six inside directors abstaining from the vote, CNA's seven outside directors picked Elmer "Nick" Nicholson, the president of Fidelity Mutual Insurance Company of Philadelphia. Scott left the company the day Nicholson was chosen.

LeRoy Botkin, a CAC actuary at the time, recalled the drama in the boardroom:

When Howard Reeder retired, most people expected that Dave Scott would be named Howard's successor as Chairman of CNAF. Because of Reeder's neutrality on the selection of his successor, a board committee recommended Elmer Nicholson, and the directors subsequently gave their approval. Dave Scott resigned immediately because he could not understand why Howard Reeder had not recommended him to the board.

Joining Continental Assurance Company in 1941 as head of the Actuarial Department, David G. Scott moved quickly through the ranks to become president of CAC in 1963. During his tenure with the company, CAC grew from $367 million in force to $9 billion, and from $40 million in admitted assets to $1 billion. Under Scott's direction, the Actuarial Department implemented Continental's simplified rate book, an innovative, agent-friendly reference manual for life underwriters.

A Mandate for Change

Nicholson felt that his status as an outsider brought with it a mandate for change. He had to move quickly to stem the losses at CNAF and he vowed to be tough. Nicholson believed in outside investment and acquisitions, but he felt that acquiring capable managers was just as important as acquiring good companies.

Nicholson attempted to sell CNA Nuclear Leasing, although he didn't succeed until 1974. He was able to trim the losses in non-insurance to $1.1 million in 1972 from $6.5 million in 1971. Nicholson also decided to reorganize the holding company into four groups — insurance, asset management, real estate and financial services. Despite the continuing drop in income, CNAF grew. CNAF acquired a new insurance distribution firm, Modern America, a Dallas-based corporation that mass marketed financial planning services, including life insurance and mutual funds.

While Nicholson focused on CNAF, profits tumbled at Continental Casualty. Despite the importance of the insurance operations to the overall financial health of CNA, CCC seemed to be adrift.

Nicholson's message to stockholders in February, 1974 summed up the economic factors negatively affecting the company: "... spiraling inflation, record-high short-term money costs ... and a tight mortgage market." Unexpected underwriting losses forced CNAF to add $53 million to Continental Casualty's reserves in 1973. CNA assured Wall Street there would be no more surprises, but CNA was forced to add another $30 million to Continental Casualty's reserves in the first quarter of 1974, $40 million in the third quarter and, finally, an additional $6 million in the fourth quarter of the year.

At the holding company level, pretax operating income dropped to $25 million in 1973 from $140 million in 1972. By 1974, the company posted a loss of $188 million.

Canadian-born Elmer L. "Nick" Nicholson was chosen from over 100 candidates to become CNAF's Chairman in 1971.

Richard Nixon's presidency reflected the

turbulent and changing times in America.

What Went Wrong?

On Monday, July 22, 1974, *The Wall Street Journal* published an article that rocked the company. Under the headline, "CNA Financial Corp., Once the Avid Hunter, Now Is Worried Prey," the *Journal* took a critical look at the company's management practices and financial strategies.

The *Journal's* analysis conceded that some of the company's problems could be attributed to outside forces, like inflation and high jury awards. But it laid most of the blame squarely at the feet of the management team. Apart from its ill-fated diversification program, analysts cited costly mistakes in the insurance operations, including poorly-planned products and unrealistic pricing. Finally, the newspaper reported that CNA's decision to pump money into the reserves for prior year losses was prompted by management's failure to set aside enough money in the first place. Many other companies would subsequently experience similar reserve deficiencies, but these problems emerged at CNA sooner compared to some of its peers.

CNA — The Prey

As a solution to the problems, Nicholson attempted a merger. In October 1973, the company agreed to be acquired by Gulf Oil Corporation in a proposed $850 million stock-and-debt deal. For Gulf, the deal would have reduced its dependence on Middle East oil at a time when the Organization of Petroleum Exporting Countries (OPEC) was becoming increasingly powerful. Less than a month after the deal was announced, though, Gulf called it off after CNA reported more reserve problems.

In the wake of the failed deal, CNA was in play. Its stock was selling for considerably less than its book value of $14 per share.

The Wall Street Journal's October 1974 article summed up CNA's troubled circumstances.

Role Reversal

CNA Financial Corp., Once the Avid Hunter, Now Is Worried Prey

Its Status as Glamour Stock Gone, Company Battles Take-Over Bid by Loews

A Second Look at the 1960s

7/22/74

By Jonathan R. Laing
Staff Reporter of The Wall Street Journal

CHICAGO—In the late 1960s, the management of CNA Financial Corp. coined a

From left to right
Larry Tisch, Ed Noha, Bob Tisch and
Lester Pollack

The Tisch brothers, their right-hand man
Lester Pollack, and Ed Noha moved
quickly, ultimately posting profits with-
in a year of Loews' takeover of CNAF.

Loews Steps In

In May 1974, the Loews Corporation — cash-rich from its profitable hotel, theater and tobacco operations — announced its intention to seek control of CNA. Loews, which was directed by brothers Laurence "Larry" and Preston Robert "Bob" Tisch, had already purchased more than five percent of the insurance giant's stock and offered to purchase another 20 million shares of common and preferred stock at $6 and $8 per share respectively.

CNA rejected the offer and a bitter fight for the future of the company began. Both sides scrambled to line up support from stockholders. Loews filed a $120 million damage suit against Nicholson and a major stockholder, the Winterthur Insurance Company. CNA countered by appealing to the Chicago City Council for legislation blocking the takeover.

Then, in October 1974, CNA announced that it had incurred a net loss of $135 million in the third quarter, including $40 million required to increase reserves. Surplus dropped dramatically — by year's end it was $117.5 million, down from $322.9 million at the beginning of the year.

The news gave Loews Chairman Larry Tisch pause. Loews immediately withdrew its bid while it studied the new financial disclosures. Within a few days, Loews revised the bid to $5 per share for the common stock and $6.75 for the preferred. CNA's board immediately accepted the offer to sell and, in December 1974, Loews officially took over the company.

Nicholson resigned within a few weeks and Larry Tisch was named chairman of the holding company, CNA Financial, with $4.4 billion in assets. Loews had acquired 51.6 percent of the company for an estimated $129 million, bringing the total Loews ownership to 56.6 percent.

Tisches Take Charge

Larry Tisch and his brother Bob had already made a career of buying undervalued companies and turning them around. Starting out with $125,000 from their father, the brothers purchased a small New Jersey hotel. With Larry crunching the numbers and Bob in charge of operations, they turned their investment into one of the nation's largest financial empires in less than two decades.

Soon after the takeover of CNA, Larry assured stockholders, "Loews believes CNAF is a sound company in the basic insurance industry with fine potential for significant progress."

CNA and Loews were a study in corporate contrasts. Loews' headquarters staff of fewer than 20 people managed $2.7 billion worth of hotel, theater and tobacco interests and exercised prudent fiscal management. CNA, on the other hand, had just built an expensive new home office building and had a top-heavy management structure. Belt-tightening — expense reduction from top to bottom — was mandated to save the company.

Noha Becomes Chairman

On February 1, 1975, a new chairman and chief executive officer took over the leadership of CNA's insurance companies. Loews recruited a seasoned insurance executive to turn CNA around — the same man Nicholson had attempted to hire for the ailing company just months before — Edward J. Noha. A 20-year veteran of Allstate, Noha held more than a dozen different jobs during his tenure there, fixing trouble spots throughout the company. By the time Loews approached him, he was executive vice president of Allstate.

A dynamic, assertive leader, Ed Noha brought with him boundless energy and unwavering confidence in CNA's potential to rise once again to the top. Noha told CNA shareholders at his first meeting with them, "I did not come to CNA to preside over the dissolution of a once mighty giant. I came here to participate in a revitalization and a re-growth that is going to result in CNA becoming a premier company in the insurance industry." Relentless in his pursuit of this goal, he put in long hours and expected the same of everyone else. If CNA was to stage a comeback, it would require a company-wide effort.

Noha's "hands-on" style energized the company. During his first few months on the job, he visited every department at the home office, introducing himself as the new chairman. He hosted coffees with company employees while soliciting their ideas. Not only did he acquaint himself with the employees, he reached out to the branch offices and the network of independent agents. Much of his time was spent on the road reinforcing relationships between the home office and field.

Of his first days at CNA Noha recalled, "There was a lot of turmoil. The entire industry was concerned as to whether CNA would make it." At the time, the company's structure was complex, unwieldy, making it difficult for agents and customers to conduct business with CNA. The company was mired in inefficiencies and unnecessary costs resulting from overlapping management and duplicate operations.

Noha was up to the challenge. His plan for CNA was simple: "completely rebuilding and reorganizing ... plugging the holes, bailing out the water and establishing a team." First obtaining a $50 million cash infusion from Loews to strengthen CNA's surplus, he next launched a massive reorganization. Frank Patalano, executive assistant to Nicholson and subsequently to Noha, recalled, "We had all the 1,800 different units of the company on pieces of paper pinned all over the conference room. Ed familiarized himself with the entire operation. That's how we put it all together. Within 16 months, Ed had combined all the insurance operations into six departments reporting directly to him." New talent was brought in from outside CNA to fill key positions. Larry Ballard took over marketing, while Jack Avignone was named head of computer operations and services. Dennis Chookaszian became vice president and corporate controller, a post that was created to provide tighter financial control at CNA.

Strengthening field operations was an integral part of Noha's restructuring strategy. A single Field Operations Department was established with direct responsibility for field offices and personnel. The 30 full-service branch offices reported to four regional vice presidents, who had full responsibility for all insurance operations within their territories. Life sales offices were relocated within branch offices, allowing for shared support systems and sales opportunities. Broader responsibility was delegated to regional and branch managers.

Edward J. Noha has a long-standing commitment to education. He worked his way through night school classes at New York City's PACE University with a job in the Manhattan offices of the United States Justice Department, commuting an hour-and-a-half from his home in the Bronx. While chairman of CNA, Noha took up the cause of quality education and continues to support educational initiatives today.

CNA boasts field offices housed in landmark buildings throughout the United States.

From left to right
Orlando, Florida
Nashville, Tennessee
New York City
Reading, Pennsylvania

CARE — a special program at CNA

In 1976, Chairman Ed Noha decided "to do something that would recognize employees … that would tell them that we care about them." The first CARE awards, recognizing distinguished performance of CNA employees, were given in May 1976. CARE award recipients are nominated by their peers and chosen by the CARE evaluation committee for their Contributions, Achievements, Results and Effort.

The program continues today. CARE awards are given for consistent, outstanding performance. CARE winners are chosen quarterly and receive, among other recognition gifts, gold rings featuring the CARE insignia. They also are invited to attend an annual banquet in their honor at the home office in Chicago. *Inside CNA,* the employee publication, regularly profiles winners, with an excerpt from their nomination letters, detailing why they are deserving of the award. More than 550 CNA employees have earned CARE awards since the program began.

Red Ink to Black

Decisive action produced swift results. In the first half of 1975, Continental Casualty posted pre-tax profits of $7 million compared to a $23 million loss the previous year.

While Noha focused on the core insurance business, the Loews management team was grappling with the legacy of diversification. Among other things, Loews sold 55 nursing homes that CNA owned and cut the staff of its home-building subsidiary to 96 from 600 people.

After one year under Loews management, CNA posted a $107 million dollar profit versus a $207 million loss in 1974. Over the next few years, CNA divested, discontinued or wrote off nearly all of its non-insurance operations, becoming an insurance company once again as it had been prior to 1968.

Left
When Noha joined CNA, he joked that the Chicago home office building would be painted green when the company returned to profitability. By 1978, Noha felt the company had improved enough to warrant the symbolic painting of the building in this Inside CNA *photograph.*

A Struggle to Survive

Even as CNA's rapid recovery was being lauded by the financial press, the property and casualty industry was experiencing the worst underwriting losses in its history — a record $3.9 billion. The industry was being battered by a seemingly never-ending barrage of financial woes. Inflation was galloping along at 15 to 20 percent, leading to increased costs. Lawsuits were increasingly commonplace — the number of product liability lawsuits jumped to 1 million in 1975 from 100,000 in 1966. Physicians in particular were besieged by malpractice claims, with medical malpractice awards soaring both in frequency and amount. Life insurance companies were moving into the property and casualty fields.

The industry, Noha warned, is in "a struggle to survive ... a struggle many companies are losing." Approximately 20 insurers failed in 1975, the year Noha was selected "Insurance Newsmaker" by the insurance editors of the *Journal of Commerce*. Noha realized that the hostile industry environment put CNA in an especially precarious position. As a company only just back from the brink of insolvency, CNA's next steps had to be chosen cautiously. While others engaged in competitive rate cutting, often to non-sustainable levels, CNA responded by choosing long-term market stability and a sound financial basis over short-term solutions.

Years of mismanagement had cost CNA its credibility with agents, customers and the financial press. That loss of confidence had translated into loss of business. Noha realized CNA's success required more than shrewd business decisions. The company had to rebuild its links to its agents and customers if it was to return to a leadership position in the industry. Noha decided that fostering a healthy relationship with independent agents had to be the first step toward that goal.

A Battle Plan for American Agents

In mid-1979 to the heroic strains of the theme from the movie "Star Wars," an appreciative audience of 250 agents watched as Darth Vader was forced to retreat in the face of the powerful CNA Life Force. The Hollywood-style excitement marked the introduction of eight new life products and a new multi-peril commercial property and liability package.

It was CNA's way of explaining to the agents that "total service" was now the key to survival. CNA would provide agents with a full range of products, allowing each of them to provide coverage for all of a client's personal and business needs. Agents would be able to sell all of CNA's insurance products at the same time.

At first, Noha admitted, communication with CNA's agents was difficult. Because he had spent his entire career with a direct writer, they had preconceived notions about him. Noha found the company's relationship with the agencies weak. "There was apathy," he told the *Chicago Sun-Times*.

To strengthen the relationship, Noha personally met with hundreds of agents. "I would share my views about CNA with them and talk about integrity and commitment. And when we made a promise, it wasn't just a promise, it was a commitment."

At the February 1986 HPA meeting in Dallas, Noha and members of his staff whooped it up with CNA's rendition of the "Super Bowl Shuffle." In January 1986, the Chicago Bears won the Super Bowl. While Coach Ditka led the Bears to victory, Noha also had a winning team in the '80s.

CNA...for all the commitments you make

Commitment is helping children learn.

The CNA Insurance Companies understand the importance of commitment. And CNA provides all kinds of insurance to help those who make commitments keep them.

INSURANCE FROM
CNA

CNA Insurance Companies/CNA Plaza/Chicago, IL 60685 • Independent agents who represent CNA are listed in the Yellow Pages

r all the commitments you make

...more precious than the time you spend with your children. Helping them learn by your example. Preparing them to face life's challenges on their own.

The CNA Insurance Companies know how important it is to be there when you're needed. We've been there for almost 100 years. Through our agents, we provide a full range of insurance protection for family, home and business. With the industry's highest A+ rating, we're a company you can count on. Helping you keep the commitments you make.

Insurance for individuals, business, groups and associations.

INSURANCE FROM
CNA

CNA Insurance Companies/CNA Plaza/Chicago, IL 60685. Independent agents who represent CNA are listed in the Yellow Pages.

These ads were part of a series that launched CNA's new corporate ad campaign in 1983. Today, the campaign's theme is the company's official tagline which is used in conjunction with the CNA wordmark.

CNA's renewed commitment to the agencies led to the creation of the High Performance Agency program (HPA) in 1978. The program addressed the agents' need for market stability, promising them "a company and a line of products they can be sure of" in exchange for writing a set volume of high quality business each year in agreed-upon lines. Noha promised his field people, "We will not walk away from an agent because of losses on the insurance he may write." CNA gave agents commission guarantees, a share in profits and fast claims adjustment. CNA also developed new products to meet the competition and launched a coordinated marketing program to support the agents, which included training to sell the full line of products, both life and casualty. Noha stressed, "Commitment is what our business is all about," and his focus on commitment permeated his tenure as CEO.

Rebuilding a National Image

For all his efforts, Ed Noha still had to reposition CNA in the minds of American consumers. CNA hadn't spent a dime on national advertising since 1973. Noha decided to budget $1 million for a new campaign.

The company's first salvo in the credibility offensive began in the insurance trade press. Four-color ads invited insurance industry leaders to take a fresh look at the new CNA. A national advertising campaign asking potential customers to "judge us by the agents who represent us" focused on seven independent agents around the nation.

CNA's next major campaign, which was introduced in 1983, embraced agents and insurance consumers but with a different focus. A campaign whose message defines CNA to the present day, it launched the corporate slogan — "For All the Commitments You Make." CNA's ads pictured parents playing with their children, people at work in offices, and Boy Scouts at camp. The print ads were designed to reflect upon the commitments people make in life — both personal and professional.

A series of radio commercials with CNA's "commitments" theme was aired across the country. The theme was also woven into all segments of the company's operations — from policyholder materials to official stationery. "For All the Commitments You Make" is a registered trademark, which continues to represent and identify CNA today.

MATHCOUNTS leads the way for future careers

MATHCOUNTS is a coaching and competition program that makes math as exciting and rewarding as student athletic events. CNA and the National Society of Professional Engineers (NSPE) created MATHCOUNTS, the first nationwide math program for junior high school students, to help increase math proficiency.

The program has its roots in an Illinois high school math competition launched by the Illinois Council of Teachers of Mathematics and financed by CNA through its corporate giving program in 1981. CNA teamed up with the math teachers, the Chicago Urban League, and the Chicago Board of Education to create a math tutorial program called MATHCOUNTS. Propelled by its success in Chicago public schools, CNA and the NSPE took MATHCOUNTS from a local effort to a national competition for junior high students in 1983.

CNA and NSPE, whose business relationship continues to this day, found mutual interest in developing math talent. Aided by the National Science Foundation, the National Council of Teachers of Mathematics, and the Math Association of America, CNA and NSPE set into motion today's program aimed at encouraging math-related careers. The program is endorsed by the U.S. Department of Education and the National Aeronautics and Space Administration.

MATHCOUNTS begins in the fall with in-class coaching and tutoring programs to prepare "mathletes" for local and regional competitions. The program culminates in the spring, with the national finals held in Washington, D.C. Thousands of volunteers, including math teachers, annually serve as competition coordinators, score keepers and judges.

Mathletes compete on teams and individually, with winners receiving prizes such as academic scholarships and computers. More than 1 million students from all 50 states, the District of Columbia, Guam, Puerto Rico, the U.S. Virgin Islands, U.S. Defense Department schools and U.S. State Department schools participate in MATHCOUNTS.

*Ed Noha, former CNA Chairman (left)
and Phil Engel, CNA's current president, with MATHCOUNTS participants
in 1991.*

These sales promotion brochures feature some of the many industry associations and trade groups whose business insurance needs are met by CNA's CAM program.

The 1980s — A Rebirth for CNA

The years between 1978 and 1984 saw the longest and most severe underwriting decline in the history of the insurance industry. A direct result of that soft market — 100 property and casualty companies declared insolvency between 1984 and 1986.

By contrast, CNA was well on its way to recovery. Loews had already given the company a vote of confidence by increasing its ownership to more than 80 percent. CNA itself now controlled about $9 billion in assets, nearly twice as much as when Loews had taken over in 1974. The turnaround was hailed as one of the most remarkable in the history of American business. *Commerce* magazine weighed in with its own analysis, "Edward J. Noha has pulled the huge CNA Insurance Companies away from financial disaster and restored the firm to one of the strongest companies in the business."

The driving force behind CNA's spectacular recovery was Noha's hand-picked management team, which included Dennis Chookaszian and Phil Engel who are still in leadership positions today, Chookaszian as CEO and Engel as president.

Among the bright spots for CNA during this period was the growth of the Professional Liability Division (PLD). PLD sought out non-traditional types of businesses and fresh marketing channels. The division protected the professional, both medical and non-medical — doctors, dentists, lawyers, architects, publishers, directors, officers — against the non-performance of their services or misconduct while performing those services.

Because of its high profit potential, PLD rapidly became one of CNA's most prominent divisions, and CNA became a leader among professional liability insurers. According to Frank

Patalano, who led PLD at the time, professional liability was a classic example of high potential risk/high potential reward. "It was a volatile, hazardous and sophisticated business. But the monetary rewards were worth the risks," said Patalano. By 1990, PLD underwriting was approaching $700 million in revenue and generating a significant portion of CNA's profit.

PLD was not the only area of the company that was contributing significantly to the bottom line in the 1980s. CNA's Commercial Affiliation Marketing (CAM) programs featured specialized coverages for trade associations and industry groups. CAM provided custom-designed, competitively priced products to trade and industry groups during a period when their membership was questioning the value of belonging to such groups. Under the direction of Tom Grzelinski, CAM saw solid growth, reaching the $1 billion dollar threshold in 1990.

By 1989, CNA ranked as the eighth largest insurance organization in the nation, up from 17th in 1975. CNA was the largest insurer in commercial affiliation marketing, the largest in architects and engineers professional liability, third largest in medical malpractice and general liability, fifth in directors and officers liability, and sixth largest in workers' compensation insurance.

As the 1990s began, CNA was not only one of America's largest insurers, it was one of the nation's strongest. All of its operations had earned the highest ratings from A.M. Best Company, a nationally recognized firm that rates the financial strength of insurance companies.

Noha Retires

In 1992, Ed Noha reached retirement age and stepped down after 17 years at the helm of the CNA Insurance Companies. He had presided over a period of extraordinary growth, but more importantly, he had rebuilt a company that had been on the verge of insolvency.

Noha went on to assume new responsibilities as head of the Chicago Economic Development Commission, leaving behind an impressive financial record. In 1974, property and casualty written premium was $714 million; in 1991, it was $6.6 billion. In 1974, life premium was $808 million, in 1991, it was $2.4 billion. In 1974, CNA Financial incurred a net loss of $183 million; 1991 net income was $612 million. In 1974, stockholders' equity was $367 million; by 1991, it exceeded $5 billion.

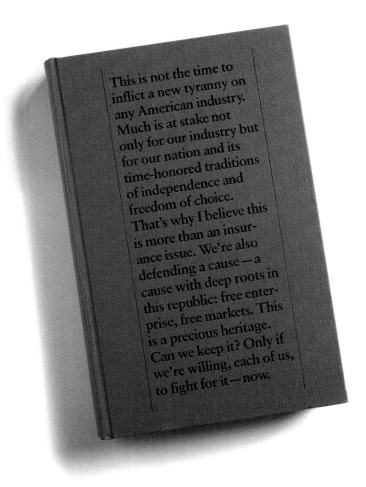

This is not the time to inflict a new tyranny on any American industry. Much is at stake not only for our industry but for our nation and its time-honored traditions of independence and freedom of choice. That's why I believe this is more than an insurance issue. We're also defending a cause—a cause with deep roots in this republic: free enterprise, free markets. This is a precious heritage. Can we keep it? Only if we're willing, each of us, to fight for it—now.

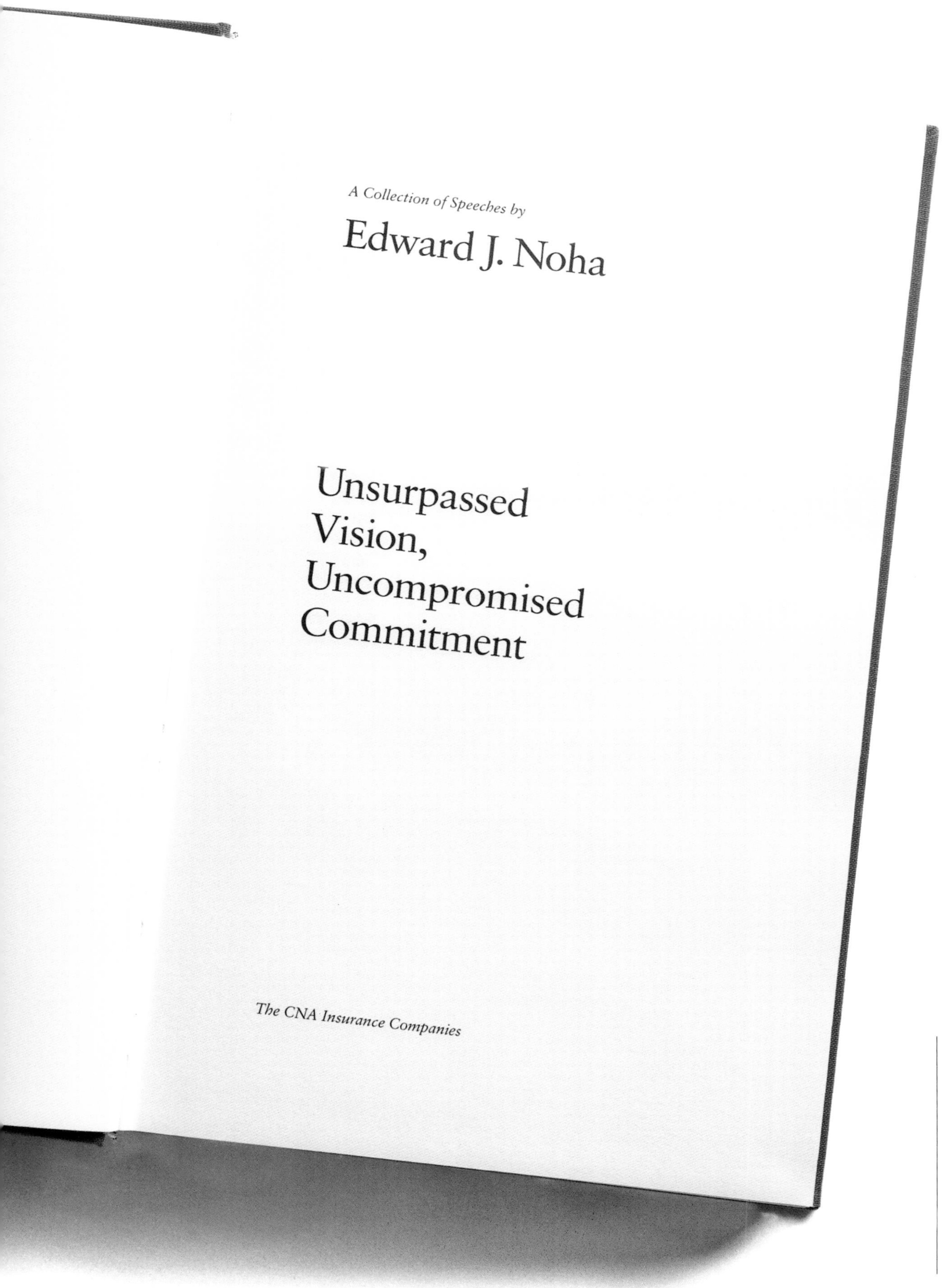

A Collection of Speeches by

Edward J. Noha

Unsurpassed Vision, Uncompromised Commitment

The CNA Insurance Companies

In May 1992 at the Spring PACER Meeting, then-President and Chief Operating Officer Dennis Chookaszian presented a specially published book for Mr. Noha to recognize his long-standing commitment to CNA. The book was a compendium of all the speeches Mr. Noha delivered throughout his career at CNA.

Chairman and Chief Executive Officer Dennis Chookaszian has emerged as a leading spokesperson in the insurance industry, particularly in the legislative arena. His calls to action reveal a keen insight into trends and challenges facing the industry.

Dennis Chookaszian: A Leader for the 1990s

CNA didn't have to look far to find a strong leader to replace Noha. Dennis Chookaszian had been with the company since 1975 and was a key member of Ed Noha's turnaround team. On September 30, 1992, the Board of Directors of CNAF elected Chookaszian chairman and chief executive officer of the CNA Insurance Companies.

With advanced degrees in chemical engineering, business and economics, Chookaszian's analytical talent and firm grasp of the insurance industry — developed over 15 years as chief financial officer of the company — had already propelled him to the post of chief operating officer and president in 1990. Prior to joining CNA, Chookaszian had been a management consultant with Touche Ross & Company (now Deloitte & Touche).

Chookaszian took the reins at a turbulent time. Revolutionary changes were occurring in the industry and the world at large. It was the beginning of an era of unprecedented technology and business applications, with the advent of mobile computers, pagers, cellular phones and modems promising to create a global workplace. The disintegration of the Soviet bloc gave added impetus to the global economy, and growing numbers of financial transactions began to take place across international borders. Chookaszian's strategic orientation and vision of the future allowed CNA to recognize the opportunities afforded by the new digital era and capitalize on them.

He realized that the insurance industry was changing too. Market pressures were forcing weak competitors out of the marketplace. Large multi-line firms were moving toward specialization and consolidation. More sophisticated insurance consumers were demanding greater efficiency and productivity. There was also heightened federal scrutiny of insurance, mandating greater involvement in the legislative reform process.

Although CNA had achieved an unprecedented recovery, the company couldn't afford to stop and savor the victory. The times demanded perceptive strategy and aggressive choices and CNA was poised to deliver.

The Fibreboard Settlement

Immediately after assuming the chairmanship, Chookaszian was called upon to make a decision crucial to CNA's future. In 1992, CNA was in the midst of a crisis. It stemmed from a $17,000 policy written for the Fibreboard Corporation in 1957. Fibreboard was a construction materials manufacturer, and many of its products contained asbestos. As asbestos-related health problems became known, billions of dollars in claims were made.

Pete Jokiel, then-chief financial officer, recalled "It became clear with some rulings in the California court system that this was not an ordinary claims situation ... this could be very large and troubling."

By the end of the fourth quarter of 1992, the Fibreboard issue had reached a critical stage, and CNA concluded that the time had come to resolve the matter. On February 8, 1993, the company announced that it would propose an all-inclusive settlement of its asbestos bodily injury litigation with Fibreboard. This was accomplished by the late fall of 1973, when CNA entered into a Global Settlement Agreement involving Fibreboard. A separate agreement, the Trilateral Settlement Agreement, was entered into by Fibreboard, CNA and Chubb so that final court approval of either of these settlement agreements would resolve all future asbestos-related bodily injury claims involving Fibreboard. CNA met its responsibility by setting aside more than $2 billion in loss reserves to meet the settlement terms.

The decision to squarely face the asbestos problem didn't come easily. As a result of the settlement, CNA Financial's shareholders' equity was substantially reduced in 1992 and 1993. The decision also negatively affected the industry ratings of CNA's property and casualty operations.

In the end, though, CNA's decision to reach a settlement brought an end to long and costly litigation. Eventually, CNA was able to absorb the losses of the settlement, while maintaining a conservative balance sheet and sound surplus and reserve positions.

Dennis Chookaszian welcomes employees to CNA's 1997 Quarter Century banquet. CNA hosts the annual affair to recognize employees celebrating 25 years or more of service with CNA.

The New Management Team

Teamwork figured prominently in Chookaszian's strategy. Consequently, he pulled together a premier management team, including individuals who participated in CNA's turnaround. Philip Engel became president of the CNA Insurance Companies in 1992. Engel had risen through the ranks since beginning his career with CNA in 1961. He is one of the few "Double Fellows" in the nation — both a Fellow of the Society of Actuaries and a Fellow of the Casualty Actuarial Society. As president, Engel manages all of CNA's staff functions and works with Chookaszian to enhance senior staff's presence inside the company and within the industry.

Today, CNA boasts a senior management team of the highest caliber. The team consists of operating heads who report to Chookaszian, and Engel's staff team, which supports the management needs of CNA's various businesses. CNA has eight business segments — commercial insurance, risk management services, specialty liability coverages, diversified lines, personal insurance, life insurance, group insurance and reinsurance. These business segments compose CNA's insurance operations and have evolved in response to changing market conditions. As a result, CNA is a broad-based insurance organization whose distribution channels cross all its business segments. Having this multi-business framework makes CNA unique. CNA's strategic management structure will continue to grow and evolve as the market continues to change and become even more competitive.

With this structure in place, CNA is prepared to embrace new opportunities and challenges. Significant changes await CNA, some predictable, some not — but as CNA proved during its first century, it has staying power. And with the right leadership, CNA will maintain its enviable reputation in the insurance industry.

The CNA Vision

In 1993, CNA's new leadership articulated the strategies, principles and goals that would set the course for a shift in CNA's operating style. It was called the CNA Vision.

Chookaszian believed that the era demanded a new way of doing business — with the leader as a facilitator, empowering people to make their own decisions. As he told *Best's Review*

The important lesson I learned was there simply isn't one way of doing things. There are many ways to accomplish an objective. Successful leaders are not doctrinaire, but rather they select a particular approach and then are very balanced and flexible in implementation.

Chookaszian introduced a new organizational structure, putting in place 30 strategic business units (SBUs). Decision-making was consolidated into each unit, with one person in charge who had full accountability for profitability. As he explained

We moved into a structure which was far more flexible. It put decision-making authority on the business unit manager's shoulders. We said to the manager: "You are in charge, so you run it."

Phil Engel functioned as CNA's agent of change. Besides the vital role he played in bringing CNA into the technological age, he was instrumental in promoting CNA's changing corporate culture — new ideas and new behaviors — to help employees keep up with the fast pace of today's dynamic work environment. He noted that

The world was changing and the company was much bigger ... the speed of events as a result of computers and telecommunications was changing. Our customers also were becoming more sophisticated. They wanted greater quality and fast customer service.

President Phil Engel has played a key role in CNA's technological advances to ensure that employees have the tools they need to enhance productivity and keep CNA competitive. Today he continues to encourage the use of cutting-edge technology, not only at CNA but throughout the industry.

Automation was a top priority and CNA was soon equipped with e-mail, voicemail and desktop computers with network applications.

The result of the CNA Vision was nothing short of a revolution in corporate culture. The CNA that emerged from the restructuring was more flexible, with quicker decision-making and greater responsiveness to customer needs. As a result, CNA continued to thrive. When Chookaszian took over in 1992, CNAF listed assets of nearly $40 billion. Just three years later, the company had hit the $60 billion mark.

Ensuring CNA's Future Success

In December 1994, CNA took the insurance industry by surprise, announcing a merger with The Continental Corporation. The merger was completed on May 10, 1995. A $1.1 billion deal, it was the first significant merger of two property and casualty companies in more than 25 years. The combination of the insurance groups formed the third largest property and casualty organization in the United States.

Chookaszian summed up the benefits in CNA's quarterly marketing magazine, *Viewpoint*:

CNA agent partners will see significantly expanded capability in lines where CNA had not previously been active, such as MOAC (Marine Office of America Corporation) and boiler and machinery. Continental agents can capitalize on CNA's strengths in workers' compensation, general liability and commercial auto.

The merger not only increased CNA's customer base but also provided greater opportunities for cross-selling products, and it gave CNA an estimated $300 million in cost reductions. The merger also enhanced CNA's global presence through CNA International — a business unit that serves American insurance needs overseas.

Acquisition was not Chookaszian's only strategy for growth. Alliances, partnerships and joint ventures were equally desirable, as long as the overall objectives were met — expanding CNA's capabilities and achieving the scale and expertise necessary for CNA to remain a world-class insurer.

Structural changes within CNA, the settlement with Fibreboard, and the merger with The Continental Corporation have enabled CNA to approach its second century revitalized — a modern company with a legacy of proven dependability and commitment. Already one of the top insurers in the nation, CNA continues to be a leader in the industry.

Transformational Ideas of the 1990s

The Continental merger, while a dramatic milestone for CNA, was only one sign of much more powerful currents of change in the insurance industry at the close of the 20th century.

Merger and acquisition activity had grown steadily. Price competition had intensified since the late 1980s, with no let-up in sight. And advances in technology opened the door to entrepreneurial ventures that would have been impractical a few years earlier.

Meanwhile, moving just below the surface is a set of business ideas with the potential to transform the way insurance products are created and distributed.

The Internet is more than an information highway. It is a growing distribution channel for insurance and a stepping-off point for new approaches to business processing and communications. Professional Employer Organizations, which take on the administrative tasks of employers, are providing a way for small businesses to gain benefits once available only to the largest employers. Insurance securitization is bridging the gap between insurance and the capital markets by creating insurance-based financial instruments.

Meanwhile, virtual insurance companies are on the horizon. Through business process outsourcing, insurance organizations can transfer their administrative functions to efficient, high-tech service companies. Banks in insurance represent another fundamental change. With regulatory barriers coming down, banks are becoming a major provider of insurance products and services.

Transformational ideas like these are changing the rules of the game. The insurance marketplace of the future will be a more rough-and-tumble, entrepreneurial arena. Today's competitor will be tomorrow's joint venture partner. In this dynamic marketplace, CNA has its sights set on a new level of success — the success of a world-class organization.

The Continental soldier

The Continental Corporation
A Historical Timeline

1853 | Issued its first policy on January 7th.

1854 | Distribution network reached 63 agents, 30 located outside of New York state.

1857 | Began issuing participating policies in order to create a loss reserve fund.

1861 | Constructed first office building at 102 Broadway across from Trinity Church graveyard.

1866 | Designated the Continental soldier as its trademark.

1871 | Suffered claims losses of $1.7 million in the Great Chicago Fire.

1874 | Built Brooklyn office building at Court and Montague Streets.

1882 | Began offering marine and tornado insurance. Three years later, began issuing hail insurance on crops.

1895 | Constructed new fireproof 12-story home office at 46 Cedar Street.

1906 | Paid $1.75 million in claims from the San Francisco Earthquake.

Board authorized $500,000 to capitalize a new company, The Fidelity Fire Insurance Company.

1910 | Fidelity Fire Insurance merged with ailing Phoenix Insurance Company of Brooklyn, creating the Fidelity-Phoenix Fire Insurance Company of New York.

1911 | Continental and Fidelity-Phoenix Insurance Companies created automobile departments and began writing auto damage insurance.

1912 | Built new offices at 80 Maiden Lane — a 25-story building designed by D.H. Burnham of Chicago.

1915 | Created the American Eagle Fire Insurance Company.

1916 | Became first insurance company traded on the New York Stock Exchange.

1918 | Continental, along with its affiliates, American Eagle Fire Insurance and Fidelity-Phoenix Insurance, became the America Fore Group.

1919 | America Fore Group participated with seven other companies in the formation of the Marine Office of America (MOA).

1929 | Acquired controlling interest in The Fidelity and Casualty Company of New York and Niagara Fire Insurance Company.

Continental's stock plummeted from $109\frac{1}{2}$ to $46\frac{1}{2}$ during the stock market crash. Paid its dividend throughout the Great Depression without interruption.

1936 | Changed name to America Fore Insurance and Indemnity Group.

1953 | Formed AFCO, a wholly-owned premium finance subsidiary empowered to finance premium written by insurance carriers.

1957 | Opened America Fore School of Insurance for agents and brokers.

Established the 80 Maiden Lane Foundation, a non-profit philanthropic organization, to support social welfare through educational and civic projects.

Acquired control of the Fireman's Insurance Company of Newark and subsidiary companies of the Loyalty Group; renamed the merged companies the America Fore Loyalty Group.

1853 | 1995

1853 – 1906

1907 – 1919

1920 – 1957

1959	Merged with Fidelity-Phoenix. The Niagara Insurance Company (Bermuda) was created in order to enter international and reinsurance markets. It later became The Security Reinsurance Corporation.
1962	America Fore Loyalty Group changed its name to The Continental Insurance Companies.
1963	Established The National Reinsurance Corporation.
1964	Played an important, double role at the 1964-1965 New York World's Fair as a major insurance underwriter and as an exhibitor. Became part owner of the Phoenix Assurance Company of London.
1965	Introduced Dial-A-Claim rapid accident reporting. Acquired Appleton & Cox and Buckeye Union Casualty. Entered the field of credit life insurance through National-Ben Franklin Life Insurance.

1958 – 1965

1966	Established Continental College Scholarship Plan for the children of employees. Merged with Boston Old Colony Insurance. Later acquired Underwriters Adjusting Company, Franklin Life Insurance Company, Diners Club, American Title Insurance, Glens Falls Insurance, The National Life Assurance Company of Canada, Kansas City Fire and Marine Insurance, Capital Financial Services, and the Pacific Insurance Group.
1968	Created a parent holding company, The Continental Corporation. Suffered a net loss of $4 million in claims rising from the arson and looting in 168 American cities following the assassination of Rev. Martin Luther King, Jr. in Memphis. Established INSCO, an information systems subsidiary, to provide computer systems and data processing services.
1969	Two subsidiaries, Marine Office of America and Appleton & Cox, merged, creating the Marine Office-Appleton & Cox (MOAC).
1972	Received approval from the Japanese government to write primary insurance and reinsurance business.

1966 – 1972

1973	Pioneered Personal Comprehensive Protection — the first nationally marketed home and auto package. Acquired interest in Puerto Rican-American Insurance and the French insurer, La Preservatrice.
1974	Opened an environmental health laboratory for industrial safety in Dallas, Texas.
1975	Acquired interest in The Insurance Corporation of Ireland. Expanded into Hawaii, Germany and Latin America.
1976	Entered the excess and surplus markets with the purchase of Unionamerica Insurance Group, which became the Swett & Crawford Group.
1977	Established Continental Reinsurance Corporation, aimed at the international reinsurance market. Sold interest in Franklin Life.
1978	Continental delegation visited the People's Republic of China. MOAC signed an agreement for People's Insurance to act as MOAC's claims agent in Chinese ports.
1981	Launched Continental Risk Services, a subsidiary marketing risk management.
1982	Purchased William Penn Life Assurance Company of America.

1973 – 1982

1983	Sold Swett & Crawford to St. Paul Fire & Marine Insurance Company, thereby exiting the wholesale brokerage business. Opened Continental Center, the new 41-story Home Office at 180 Maiden Lane.
1987-89	Decided to focus on property and casualty insurance. Exited the life and health businesses.
1989	Exited the life insurance arena with the sale of the William Penn Companies. Paid claims of $230.6 million on damage caused by Hurricane Hugo.
1992	Won Catalyst Award for the Advancement of Women.
1993	Ranked the 11th largest U.S. property and casualty company based on 1993 premium volume. Assets totaled $16.1 billion. Saved customers $60 million through medical cost containment initiatives in the workers' compensation area.
1995	Acquired by CNA for $1.1 billion on May 10, forming the sixth largest U.S. insurance group.

1983 – 1995

New Ventures and Alliances

The road to world-class performance starts with profitable growth — no small challenge in the mature U.S. insurance market. But just months into its 100th year, CNA solidified its reputation as a visionary company with a range of growth initiatives that capitalize on transformational business ideas. They include

The launch of CNA UniSource, a Professional Employer Organization that provides employers with payroll, risk management and human resource services.

Active exploration of insurance securitization with the creation of Hedge Financial Products.

Investment in InsWeb, the Internet gateway to the insurance industry, as well as the development of a CNA site on the World Wide Web.

An alliance with Computer Sciences Corporation (CSC) to form a new outsourcing service for the various business processes of life insurance companies.

Banking initiatives — both agency-community direct partnerships and alliances with larger nationally-oriented banks — to participate in the growth of banks in insurance.

Independent Capital Structures

Not only will the CNA of the next century be larger, it will have a financial infrastructure better suited to a dynamic environment of unknown risks and unexpected opportunities.

Until the 1990s, CNA's capital structure was like its management structure — highly centralized. All the businesses were supported by one capital structure. By the end of 1997, CNA had four independent capital structures for different businesses. Over time, more of these structures will be formed. Some will operate as separately capitalized companies, with CNA retaining strategic control.

This new financial infrastructure will reinforce the idea of accountability, giving managers more control of the capital that supports their business. Independent capital structures will also provide more flexibility to form partnerships and to finance acquisitions. In addition, CNA will be better protected from unusual losses in any of its businesses.

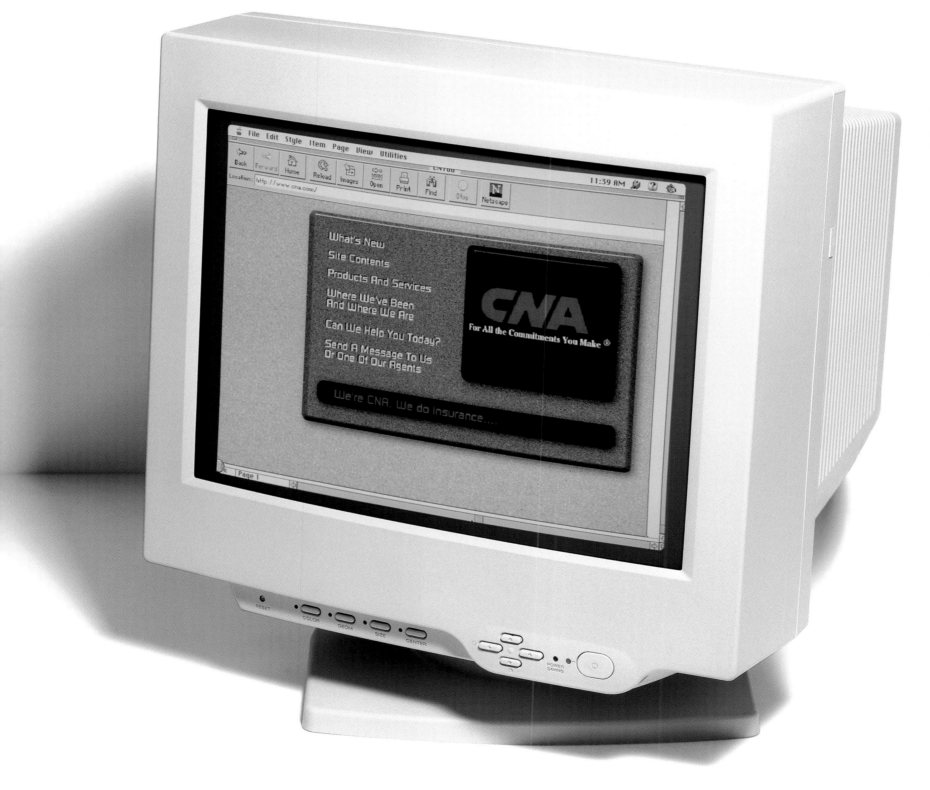

"Our challenge is to build on the legacy

of the past for an even brighter future."

— Dennis Chookaszian

Collaborative Partnerships

In a time of specialization and the break-up of multi-line insurance companies, CNA is not following the competition down this road. Instead, the SBUs and the independent capital structures are focusing on the advantages of being part of a multi-business organization. They share customers, skills and distribution systems to gain an edge over more narrowly focused competitors.

To maximize this advantage, CNA is emphasizing the idea of collaborative partnerships at all levels of the organization. Partnership among CNA employees enables them to achieve business objectives while also realizing a sense of personal satisfaction and growth. That positive experience is vital for sustaining peak performance over time.

Collaboration also includes building strong relationships with business partners and customers. In a complex and unpredictable business environment, these relationships increase CNA's ability to add value and capitalize on the opportunities of change.

The next 100 years will be an exciting century for the insurance industry and for CNA. With growth initiatives underway, a more flexible financial structure in the works and an organization driven by the spirit of partnership, CNA is on its way to a world-class future.

A Second Century of Success

Today, the year 2097 seems unimaginable. One hundred years ago, 1997 would have seemed equally inscrutable to the founders of a small company, modestly housed in a two-room office. Could those founders have imagined that a century later the company would not only still exist, but would have attained a position of preeminence within the insurance industry? With more than $60 billion in assets, 400 office sites and 20,000 employees worldwide, modern-day CNA is barely recognizable as that fledgling Detroit-based insurer. Still, CNA's heritage is evident in the company's spectacular growth and continued success. Its solid foundation has been built on 100 years of dedication and service as well as the business acumen of its leaders, business partners and employees.

At the dawn of its second century, CNA remains a leader in the insurance industry, thanks to a legacy of innovation and the ability to meet the changing needs of its customers.

The changes the future will bring — in the industry, in technology, in life — are unpredictable. What remains certain is CNA's dependability in times of change and CNA's core values: commitment, stability and financial strength. They are CNA's foundation and will continue to stand the test of time.

Acknowledgements

A number of people and organizations have given generously of their time and skills to the successful completion of this book, "CNA: A Century of Commitment." Their contributions are deeply appreciated. Special thanks to Dennis Chookaszian and Philip Engel for their vision, perspective and direction and to CNA employee Pamela Lyons for her oversight and management of the book's development.

Debra Tadevich of Tadevich & Associates in New York conducted research and the story direction. Bruce Hagan was the writer. Kerry Grady and Tom Zurawski of Grady, Campbell, Incorporated, Chicago were the book designers. Original studio photography was created by François Robert.

All archive material was provided by CNA. Historical photographs are part of collections owned by Corbis-Bettman, FPG and Photonica.

Appreciation is further extended to employees, former employees, retirees and business partners who contributed historical documents, memorabilia and stories to CNA's Centennial book and permanent archives.

Colophon

This special edition of "CNA: A Century of Commitment" is published by CNA. First editions were printed in the fall of 1997.

The typeface used for this volume is Monotype *Bulmer*, designed by William Martin and used by the printer, William Bulmer, circa 1790. It was electronically typeset using Apple Macintosh computers.

This book was printed on six-color Heidelberg presses by the Hennegan printing company in Cincinnati, Ohio. The text paper is Potlatch Eloquence and the end sheets are Weyerhauser's Cougar Opaque. This volume is casebound by BindTech in book cloth by Brillianta.